Case Studies in Business Planning

2ND EDITION

Bill Richardson · Anthea Gregory
John Patterson · Susan Leeson

Sheffield Business School,
Management Strategy and Business Decision-Making Team

Pitman

Pitman Publishing
128 Long Acre, London WC2E 9AN

A Division of Longman Group UK Limited

First published in 1989
Second edition published in 1992

British Library Cataloguing in Publication Data
A catalogue record for this book is available from the British Library

ISBN 0 273 03722 6

Printed in Great Britain by The Bath Press, Avon

Contents

SECTION 4   PUBLIC SECTOR ORGANISATIONS

SECTION 5   FINANCIAL SERVICES

SECTION 6 INDUSTRIAL PRODUCTS

*Sample topics covered – note that practically all the cases lend
themselves to a consideration of environmental change and the changing
nature of environments.

The case studies in this book are intended to be aids to student learning
rather than comments on the handling of particular business situations.

Preface

Plans and decisions are the vital prerequisites to the actual work performed by organisations. Business success depends upon successful planning and decision-making. The organisation itself is a strategy for the attainment of desired futures – for all those who interact with it. All those plans and decisions, which the organisation undertakes and implements, together contribute to the success of the organisation as a strategy.

At the heart of university, polytechnic and college business studies/ organisation studies type courses and subjects, is the quest to improve students' planning/decision-making skills. This underlying aim applies across the full range of diploma, certificate, degree and post-graduate courses and to all students – whether full time, part time, in or out of employment. Increasingly practising managers are looking for help towards the improvement of their decision-making skills.

At Sheffield we view Strategy (with a capital 'S') as the organisation itself – a mechanism for creating wealth and offering satisfactions to people who interact with it. The successful organisation breeds wealth and satisfies aspirations as it moves through its environments over time. *All* the plans, decisions and activities made and implemented by the organisation impact on the levels of strategic success achieved, ie *Strategy* making is much more than the making of those major product/market choices implementations which form the subject matter of many corporate strategy type programmes of study. This book and its sister publication, *Business Planning*, are intended to help improve skills across the range of organisational planning activities.

This book is intended for use with these central decision-making units. It is a book containing case studies which can be used across the range of decision making subjects through the life of student programmes of business studies.

For practitioners of business this book provides models of business problems, and approaches to business problems, which might hopefully provide vehicles for learning how more customised plans and decisions might be better made. In consultancy and management development situations our staff and clients find the theory of management strategy to be an invaluable source of assistance.

A case study is a written description of an organisation. The primary reasons for using a case study for business education are to enable the student to see how actual organisations have performed the strategic management process and to allow students to practice and develop their skills in applying strategic management concepts to actual organisations. The cases in this book have already been used at Sheffield for this purpose. They have been created from material taken from real organisations. While in some instances the identities of these organisations have been disguised, nevertheless, students should be aware that the problems addressed in the case studies *are* real. We hope that this one book encapsulates enough 'real' organisational problems and activities to provide a continuous source of fruitful material – to assist in the study of organisation planning and decision making throughout the life of the students' decision making studies.

This book has a sister text *Business Planning: An Approach to Strategic Management*, second edition, W Richardson and R Richardson, Pitman Publishing, 1992, which can be used to advantage as a complementary medium for the teaching and learning of strategic planning.

Acknowledgements are due to colleagues who have provided material for this book and who are identified in the contents pages. Special thanks are due to Maurice Brown, Collette White, Janet Kirkham, Dick Gadsden, Nick Foster, Graham Worsdale, Ken Roberts, Roger Hawkins and Peter Lawless who have helped test and improve the material. Last but not least, we offer our thanks to students and business colleagues, past and present for their contributions to this book and to our personal development.

Bill Richardson
John Patterson
Anthea Gregory
Susan Leeson

Members of the Strategy and Decision-Making Team,
Sheffield City Polytechnic

Section 1 · Retailing

1 · Chrissie's Cakes

Anthea Gregory

Chrissie's Cakes was founded in 1984 by Chrissie Fox. The company initially employed five people and operated from a single industrial unit in the suburbs of London. Chrissie had spent many years, prior to starting her own company, running a successful cake manufacturing operation only a few miles away.

When the company started it produced a limited range of products which were distributed by the company to London caterers and restaurants. Things soon changed, however. Chrissie showed tremendous flair for product development and the product range rapidly increased, as did the company's customer base. The products were seen as innovative in a market that had not really developed since the discovery of the Black Forest gateau.

By 1987 the company employed 71 people (7 clerical staff, 58 production staff, 2 supervisors, 2 stores people, a production manager and a sales representative). The factory had also had to take on two additional industrial units and sales had been increasing at an exponential rate. It was at the beginning of this year that Chrissie realised that things could no longer continue as they had.

Existing customers were demanding increasingly high hygiene standards which could not be met in the existing industrial units, eg under floor drainage, sealed walls, temperature control, etc. Also the natural progression for the company was to enter retail cake manufacture. Again high standards of manufacture would be required (it was at this time that there were a growing number of food scares) and due to the volume of production necessary to enter this market the present production facility would be unable to cope. The equipment at the factory was old and very labour intensive and yet there was insufficient room to install modern equipment which could cope with the level of production required for the retail market.

Also at this stage Chrissie was finding it impossible to manage the company. She was solely responsible for all product development, a full-time job in itself, but also she was responsible for the day-to-day running of the factory. Chrissie spent a lot of time in the factory itself, especially when there was pressure to get the product through the door. She was quite a taskmaster and when she said 'jump' things happened. Unfortunately the production manager was not as forceful as Chrissie and although well liked on the factory floor was unable to get people to work to their full capacity. Chrissie realised that if the company grew any more she would be unable to cope with the workload.

The plans are made

Chrissie decided that it would be necessary to move to a new factory. She soon appreciated that the company would have to move away from London as land and property prices were at a premium. Further she decided that the company should have a purpose-built factory as the comparative cost of purchasing a factory shell and converting it to meet production and hygiene requirements was very similar and a good deal more problematic. She found a greenfield site in an enterprise zone whose previous industrial base had been steel, which had now declined. The land was relatively cheap and employment grants and loans at preferential rates were available to the company.

Plans were soon underway and costs were estimated for the building of a new factory and budgets were forecast for the company. The budgets and previous profit and loss accounts can be seen in Appendix 1.1. Although the company was growing very quickly and loans would be available, in order to build the type of factory she wanted substantial sums of money would still be required. Therefore, in 1987 Chrissie started to look for an investor for the company. Alan Brown, who knew Chrissie from her previous job, put forward funds and took a 50 per cent share in Chrissie's Cakes. It was decided that Alan would not take an active role in the company but act as chairman on the board of directors.

With this backing Chrissie was now in a position to go to the bank for additional funding. The bank was very interested in the project and made available the rest of the finance which had been projected as being required.

The site which was chosen had a number of factors in its favour. It was in the Midlands with easy access to the Ml and Al, thus making distribution to existing national catering customers easier and it was also suitable for distribution to the multiple retailers, which the company wished to supply. Also employment had always been a problem in London. Low unemployment meant wage rates were high and the retention of good staff was difficult. The consequence of this was that labour turnover was excessive and that training was often neglected. At the proposed site, though, unemployment was high and wage rates were much lower.

The new factory

By January 1989 the new factory was finally complete after a number of difficulties. The building contractors went into liquidation during its building and the net result was that the building went approximately £2m over budget and the opening was delayed by six months. This necessitated the borrowing of a further £1.5m from the bank and Alan Brown made a personal loan to the company of £0.5m. However, when complete, the factory was the most modern food production unit in the UK, possibly in Europe. The latest equipment had been carefully selected from all over Europe and the USA and it had all the features required to meet even the most exacting of hygiene standards. The offices and staff facilities were equally impressive (all micro-blinds, attriums and potted palms).

The management structure

Chrissie appreciated that the expanded company would require a more formal management structure. Hence she employed a number of managers to undertake key roles and functions within the company. The structure that emerged is shown in Appendix 1.2.

Most (though not all) of these managers were relatively young but all had some managerial experience. Chrissie wanted an enthusiastic, highly motivated, career-orientated team which she could mould and train up, rather than more experienced managers who might be less flexible and have commitments outside of their work. She paid her managers very high salaries but in return she expected hard work and total dedication.

The retailers come marching in

Before the completion of the factory the large multiple retailers had heard of Chrissie's Cakes. Soon all the major merchandisers were making regular trips to the factory site to check on the progress of the factory. One of the most prestigious retailers started to ask for new product ideas a full year before the opening of the new factory. These were developed; a German apple cake and an American cream pie. An agreement was made at the end of 1988 as to the specification, price and product launch date (this being April 1989).

The sales projections for the range had been very good. So Chrissie offered the range at a very competitive price based on costings she had made (see Appendix 1.3).

The launch

At the beginning of February 1989 the factory officially opened. The London units had built up stocks of product which were kept in outside storage in order to act as a buffer whilst the new factory got on its feet. The first day was chaos. All the new staff had been told to arrive at the beginning of their shifts to start their training. However, there were not enough managers to conduct the training and sort out the problems which kept cropping up, eg. running out of uniforms, people not knowing where they should be.

After three months things calmed down but the company still had some major problems. The training given to staff had been piecemeal. Labour turnover had been high due to the disorganisation of the first few weeks. As a result production requirements were not met and corners were being cut in the production process. Consequently there were a large number of rejects from production and many customer complaints about substandard products and unfulfilled orders. Further to this some of the equipment which had been installed was found to be unsuitable for the task at hand and the outcome was continual breakdowns which further reduced output. In London the production process had been very flexible small batch. The company tried to replicate this in its new factory but the new equipment only operated efficiently on large batches of product.

Management also had a number of difficulties. The plans that had been made prior to the move had gone out of the window on day one and the subsequent fire-fighting that ensued meant no one had time to revise the plans in order to get operating and control systems off the ground. This had serious repercussions. It meant that staff were getting used to 'muddling through' and hence they resisted or disregarded systems as management tried to introduce them.

Also when Chrissie saw problems on the factory floor she would insist on going down and sorting them out herself. Sometimes her methods contradicted those of her managers, which in due course undermined their authority and credibility. Soon morale was very low. Due to the problems of opening the new factory, production of the new retail products had to be delayed. The new launch date was set for the beginning of June 1989 but as yet no production trials had taken place.

What to do?

At the beginning of May an emergency meeting was called for all managers and directors. Chrissie had put forward an agenda and requested reports from a number of the managers. Below is a summary of the comments made by the various managers during their reports.

The accountant's report

Management accounts – 'I have been looking at our performance compared to the budgets and there are a number of areas where we are under performing. The results are as follows. Sales are 30 per cent below the budget at this stage. Raw materials usage is running at 55 per cent of revenue whereas we budgeted for 45 per cent. Production wages are running at 25 per cent of revenue whereas we budgeted for 18 per cent. The other items in the profit and loss are just about on budget. However, raw materials and wages are by far our largest costs and so this is having a serious effect on our profitability. Also the move to the factory has greatly increased our fixed costs and in order that these are covered we need to ensure we meet our turnover targets.'

Cash flow – 'Our cash flow position is very poor. We are currently at the limit of our overdraft facility with the bank. I am sure they will be reluctant to extend this any further, given that we increased the size of our loan during the building of the factory.'

The production manager's report

Productivity – 'We are still having problems in this area. I have to rely on the supervisors to get the employees to work hard but they don't seem capable of achieving this. When we were recruiting the supervisors looked good from their CVs and at the interviews, but in reality they are no better than the rest of the people on the factory floor. I think this may be partly due to their backgrounds. Most of our employees are ex-steel workers and have only worked for a large organisation. They seem to be used to having some slack built into production but that isn't the case here. It is important that everyone pulls their own weight.'

'I believe another cause of low productivity is high labour turnover. We have almost given up training now as people seem to leave as soon as they are trained. We have a core of people who are capable of carrying out the skilled tasks so we give new people the unskilled jobs where they can do least damage. If they then stay for more than a couple of weeks, we tell them we will train them for one of the higher paid skilled jobs once we have time.'

Quality – 'I know what the products should look like but I can't seem to get it across to the people on the shop floor. Sometimes I think they just don't care, they are quite happy if the cakes are lop-sided, badly decorated or undersized just so long as they can get them into their boxes. Even when they see things are obviously going wrong they don't tell me. By the time I find out the whole batch has been ruined or, even worse, I only know something has gone wrong when a customer rings up to complain.'

'The quality controllers are no better. I see them weighing and measuring things, checking them against their recipes and specifications (an example of which is in Appendix 1.4) but I never see the information. Also even they do not identify when there are quality failures. For example I was in the cake decorating area the other day and one of them stopped production. This was so they could adjust the deposit weight of the topping on our chocolate cake. This may seem reasonable but it turned out the adjustment was so small that it would make no significant difference to the final product. As a result there were 60 people doing nothing for ten minutes. But more importantly they didn't notice that the sponges were over baked and hence too dry to use. This meant that the previous hour's work was wasted. When I asked why the sponges hadn't been checked they said that it wasn't on the specification so they didn't think it was important.'

'When we started up in the new factory I thought the technical manager was going to take responsibility for quality and the quality controllers but the results so far have been very poor.'

The goods inward/purchasing manager's report

Materials usage and stock control – 'I devised a really good system for the issuing and monitoring of stock but production seem incapable of making it work. It is quite simple really. Each night I take the production plan and enter this into the computer. It calculates what raw materials are required to produce the number of products on the plan. I then get a requisition sheet which I give to the stores people. They then put all the raw materials required into the deboxing area for use the next day. The requisition is taken from the stock levels (this is done automatically by the computer based on the production plan) and all I have to do then is enter any goods received onto the computer. The computer then calculates the stock levels and compares these to the minimum allowable stock levels. It then prints out what materials will need ordering the next day. This is simple, if it weren't for production. Every day they seem to disregard the production plan. Sometimes they add products to the list, but more frequently they knock things off. The consequence is raw materials have to be put back into stock or, sometimes, extra materials will be taken out. By the time they've finished I have no idea how much stock there is and, more importantly, what the usage is. We aren't even sure if the usage figures in the computer are correct. But until I get some feedback from production as to what they have made and used, there is no way I can carry out any form of usage analysis.'

The sales manager's report

Customer relations – 'Life is difficult for me at the moment. I've got to the stage now where I don't want to answer the phone as I know it will be just another complaint. I told our customers that when we moved they could expect nothing but the best from us. I thought we would have spare capacity and so would not have to short customers on their orders. I also believed that all our new staff were going to be trained to a high standard and that we were going to instigate a "quality assurance" programme in order that our quality would be improved. However, things are far worse than they were before and from what the production manager has just said I am not convinced that things are likely to improve in the near future.'

'At present our customers are far from happy with our performance and if there isn't a drastic improvement soon I am certain we will lose customers. We can ill afford to do this given the current short fall on the sales target.'

'So far as potential new business is concerned it is terribly difficult to go out there and sell at the moment when I know we are unable to satisfy our present customers. If I go to see a large new client I try to be positive. I tell them that we can satisfy their every need but I know it will not happen and some people are bound to catch onto my lack of conviction. To be frank there are no potential new customers on the immediate horizon.'

The factory manager's report

Preparations for the new product range – 'There are a number of things we need to look at and I shall address each of these in turn. I've been looking at ways in which we can manufacture these products. I believe in order to achieve a consistent finish we need to buy a depositor (a machine which pumps out cream volumetrically) to deposit the cream topping. There are two reasons for this. First, it will reduce product handling and hence damages and, second, it will help control the usage of cream on the finish. I have been looking at two machines and have managed to collect some information on their relative costs. I hope the accountant will be able to carry out some form of analysis on this information for me to determine which is the better investment (see Appendix 1.5).'

'I am still rather worried about whether we can in fact produce these products. It is only one month from the launch and I fear we are still not ready for it. We have problems getting our normal production out, but from the beginning of June we are expecting to double output over night (in terms of numbers of cakes produced). I think it is essential that we plan the next month carefully otherwise we could jeopardise our new retail contract.'

Chrissie's overview/summary

'Well what can I say? I am very disappointed in all of you – you are all absolutely clueless! I pay you all damned good money and what do I get in return? I can see that there is no alternative but for me to come down to the factory floor and show you how it is done, yet again. You've not got any idea how to get people to do what you want!'

Appendix 1.1 *Actual and budgeted profit and loss for Chrissie's Cakes*

	31/12/86 (Actual) (£000s)	31/12/87 (Actual) (£000s)	31/12/88 (Actual) (£000s)	31/12/89 (Budgeted) (£000s)	31/12/90 (Budgeted) (£000s)
Sales	970	1527	3540	9442	12540
Deduct cost of goods sold:					
Raw materials	437	725	1735	4250	5643
Production wages	205	355	885	1700	2257
Light, heat and power	20	23	39	120	140
Consumables	33	47	62	136	165
Total cost of goods sold	695	1150	2721	6206	8205
Gross profit	275	377	819	3236	4335
Deduct:					
Establisment costs					
Rent and rates	25	26	26	66	70
Repairs	1	2	4	36	40
Distribution costs					
Distribution wages and salaries	18	26	38	200	220
Lorry fuel	16	18	40	68	72
Admin costs					
Admin salaries	15	17	20	90	99
Admin expenses	8	12	14	80	88
Sales salaries	15	16	35	76	83

10 Retailing

	31/12/86 (Actual) (£000s)	31/12/87 (Actual) (£000s)	31/12/88 (Actual) (£000s)	31/12/89 (Budgeted) (£000s)	31/12/90 (Budgeted) (£000s)
Management salaries	54	58	100	150	165
Insurance	3	3	3	20	20
Advertising	5	10	15	60	30
Financial costs					
Bank charges and interest	–	4	154	310	256
HP interest	2	2	15	26	26
Interest on shareholders loans	–	–	–	45	45
Interest on EEC loan	–	–	45	90	90
Depreciation					
Vehicle depreciation	1	1	3	30	30
Equipment depreciation	4	4	126	534	534
Total expenses	167	199	638	1881	1868
Profit/(loss)	108	178	181	1355	2467

Notes
1 Many of the costs of the new factory were incurred in 1988.
2 It is assumed the new factory will be more efficient, hence the reduction in labour and raw materials as a percentage of sales.
3 Inflation has been estimated at 10 per cent.

Appendix 1.2 *Organisational Chart of Chrissie's Cakes*

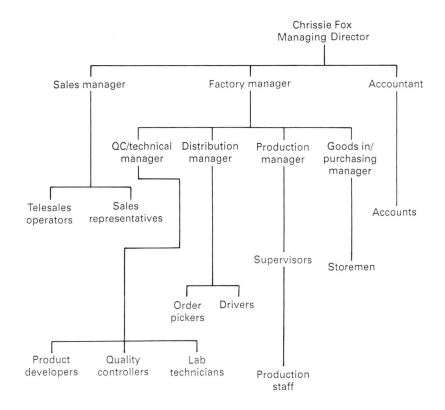

Appendix 1.3 *Costings for the new product ranges*

American cream pie

Component	Weight (kg)	Cost per kg/unit	Cost
Pastry base	0.150	0.25	0.04
Filling	0.275	0.60	0.17
Cream topping	0.075	1.75	0.13
Foil base	1	0.13	0.13
Box	1	0.12	0.12
Total materials cost			0.59
Labour cost (40 per cent of materials cost)			0.24
Total variable cost			0.83
Overhead allocation (20 per cent of total variable cost)			0.17
Total cost			1.00
Profit margin (50 per cent of total cost)			0.50
Selling price			£1.50

German apple cake

Component	Weight (kg)	Cost per kg/unit	Cost
Sponge	0.150	0.35	0.05
Fresh apple	0.175	0.65	0.11
Filling	0.100	0.53	0.05
Cream topping	0.075	1.75	0.13
Cake board	1	0.09	0.09
Box	1	0.12	0.12
Total materials cost			0.55
Labour cost (40 per cent of materials cost)			0.22
Total variable cost			0.77
Overhead allocation (20 per cent of total variable cost)			0.15
Total cost			0.92
Profit margin (50 per cent of total cost)			0.46
Selling price			£1.38

Assumptions made:

1   Materials – The materials usage is derived from the target weights from the specifications for these products.
2   Labour – At present (in the London factory) labour costs are currently running at 50 per cent of material costs for the existing product ranges. It is believed the new factory will be more efficient hence labour costs have been calculated at 40 per cent of materials cost.
3   Overhead – Overheads are allocated at the rate of 20 per cent of total variable costs.
4   Profit margin – A profit margin of 60 per cent of total costs is normal but in order to keep our price competitive this has been reduced to 50 per cent.

Appendix 1.4 *German apple cake specification * new product ***

Product code: G013

Component code	Description	Target weight (g)	Tolerance (+/- g)	Target height (mm)	Tolerance (+/- mm)
9001	Sponge (white)	150	15	70	7
A261	Fresh apple	175	18	20	2
6332	Filling	100	10	10	1
C100	Cream	75	8	10	1
Totals		500	51	110	11

Appendix 1.5 *Information on the cream depositing machines*

The two machines which are capable of depositing the cream topping for our new products are the Spondex and Grodex.

Initial costs:	The Spondex costs £120,000 and the Grodex £80,000. Both could be installed immediately.
Operations:	The machines operate slightly differently. The Spondex uses air pressure to force the deposit of cream out whilst the Grodex relies on mechanical pressure. As a consequence of this they require different amounts of labour and they have different wastage and output rates.
Labour requirements:	In order for the Spondex to operate it must always be full. So it will require one operator to fill it and one to operate the deposit. The Grodex on the other hand can be filled and operated by one operator only.
Throughput:	Because the Grodex is operated and filled by only one person it's throughput is less than the Spondex as there will be times when the operator has to fill the machine and therefore cannot be operating the deposit. The output of the machines as a result of this is as follows: Grodex: 200 deposits per hour Spondex: 300 deposits per hour
Labour costs:	Operators earn £3.50 per hour. The factory is open 5 days per week for 50 weeks of the year.
Demand:	The new customer will require 750 of each of the two new products per day, excluding Sundays. The factory will have to produce extra product and freeze it to cover demand when the factory is closed. Each product requires one deposit of cream.
Wastage:	At the start of a production run the first 2kg of cream from the Grodex are wasted as it is unusable (none is wasted with the Spondex). At the end of a production run cream will still be in the equipment and will have to be cleaned out. With the Grodex this means that 3kg are wasted but with the Spondex only 0.5kg are wasted.
Maintenance:	The suppliers of the Spondex will maintain their equipment for free for six years (this is the anticipated life of the equipment). The suppliers of the Grodex require a maintenance charge of £5,000pa. They state that the Grodex should have a useful working life of 6 years also.
Scrap value:	It is forecast that the Grodex will be worth £6,000 and the Spondex £10,000 at the end of their useful working lives.
Cost of capital:	The company's cost of capital is 15 per cent.

2 · High Street Electricals plc

Bill Richardson

This case study is intended as an aid to class discussion, rather than as a comment on the handling of a business situation.

The 1982 position

'As we approached the task of turning the company around we could see clearly a number of major problems that required urgent attention. They were all symptoms of the general malaise of a national organisation being run in an introverted, traditional, family way.'

In 1982 it was obvious to the newly incumbent management team at High Street Electricals plc (HSE) that drastic changes were required. The situation was daunting. The 1982 annual accounts showed losses of almost £4m against turnover of £42m. Massive cash injections were also needed urgently. Net debts consistently running around £10m had been a constant headache and had generated crippling interest charges.

Despite interventions by the Office of Fair Trading back in 1978 when the company had demanded unauthorised rental charge increases in breach of contracts, customer relations and practices had not improved. The organisation was not anti-social so much as apathetic to the needs and demands of its external stakeholders. Success achieved in the 'heady' days of 'Barberism' and TV sales booms had bred false confidence. The organisation was no longer effective at earning a living from an increasingly turbulent, hostile and mature market. (Information on market shares and conditions can be gleaned from the text and from Appendices 2.1 and 2.2.)

Inside the organisation, further significant problems were apparent. Control was poor. Branch managers were effectively running, in their own way, their particular business units. Senior and middle management did not talk much to each other. Sales staff and service departments did not always co-operate. Motivation was low. Resources with which to instigate changes were patently scarce. Earlier successes had facilitated and disguised the building up of inefficiencies within the organisation.

The new management

Since its foundation in 1897 HSE had been owned and managed by members of the Jameson family. The crises of the late 1970s and early 1980s, however, had resulted in the installation of a new chairman, John Fellows (who brought with him a useful track record with a variety of electrical industry companies) and a new managing director, David Monks. David Monks had previously been employed by an HSE competitor (Rumbelows Ltd). In his early 40s he was perceived to have the necessary marketing and leadership qualities to lead the HSE 'turnaround'. David recruited former Rumbelows colleagues Simon Sparkes, Andrew Fieldsend and Peter Jordan to head the organisation's finance, operating systems and marketing functions, respectively. Together with Roy Sunders, a long-serving HSE executive, this group of people comprised the HSE top strategic team. Together they quickly set about remedying the problems facing HSE.

Product/market operations

Rent or sell?

A root problem for the company was provided by its major product/market strategy – TV (and other electrical goods) *rentals* ...

'Our branch managers were geared towards pushing *new* rental agreements with *old* customers. New sets were going out over longer periods for the same weekly rental payments. All we were getting in return for the new and costly sets were the old secondhand ones. We also felt that the market was moving against rentals generally and that before long there would be room for perhaps only two major rental companies. Recent mergers tend to have confirmed our judgement of that time.'

A new strategy was implemented. HSE needed to become a *retailer* not a *renter*. By 1985 rental contribution to turnover was down from 50 per cent to less than 10 per cent. Rental remains available in some branches but where possible staff now *sell* goods on cash or credit terms. The sale of a portfolio of rental accounts in 1982 (to VisionHire for £4m cash) fitted the new strategic direction and provided a vital injection of liquidity.

Geographic areas of operation and distribution

Forty HSE stores were disposed of (all south of Oxford) with the intention of 'reducing borrowings (£4m sales price), stabilising trade and operating in a tight geographical area' (Chairman's Report, 1982). A sprinkling of southern stores has been maintained to preserve a national image (in 1986 HSE was promoting itself as 'Britain's biggest electrical independent'). Strong market position, however, is enjoyed only in HSE's home county. A total of around 100 branches is maintained but within this total figure relocation policies mean that new branches are regularly replacing older ones ...

'Many of our branches just weren't big enough to stock the items we wanted to sell. We have been disposing of our smaller, village premises as suitable alternative sites – and the necessary finance – have become available. (Although new sites are leased it still costs around £400,000 to open a large store.) We have been opening bigger and better town centre branches and "out of town" superstores.'

Recent superstore openings had been made at Leicester, Buxton and, for the first time in Lancashire, at Bolton.

A systematic refurbishment programme was also implemented. The aim here was to lift the image of the company into the 1980s and 1990s through a more futuristically designed sales outlet utilising a distinctive colour scheme and HSE 'uniformed' staff. Visits around the HSE chain in 1987 confirmed this transitionary position. Older outlets were either in the process of, or getting ready for their refits and alignment with the modern 'HSE – buy better electric' image (and away from their traditional 'HSE – friend of the family' stance).

Products and buying policies

HSE stocks a range of popular 'brown' and 'white' goods (see, for example, the products listed in Appendix 2.3). 'We used to have to try and sell a load of garbage, really', explained one branch manager. 'I think that top management felt that they couldn't get the terms they wanted from the popular manufacturers. It's different now though. We stock what the customers want – the better quality merchandise – and we often "knock the spots off" competition in price terms. Yesterday I took a walk around a local department store that always seemed to have *the* merchandise. We now match them product for product and can beat them easily on price. Our buyers check things out well and the directors personally inspect new lines before they are introduced.... We also have fewer problems with defective goods. It makes sense, I suppose. Some years ago when we also sold lower priced furniture we used to have even more problems with product quality and customer complaints.'

David Monks commented on the product/buying situation: 'Buying policies were woefully inadequate. Personal contacts between directors and suppliers counted far more than quality or customer appeal product characteristics. The company was an "easy touch" for some manufacturers and it had been over-buying.' Everyone seemed in accord over the new move towards this acquisition and sale of popular branded goods. The more recent moves of a major (and market leader) competitor – Dixons – towards the supply of its own brands was, however, already being viewed with some apprehension. Dixons' ability to buy in huge quantities and then sell at very low prices was also giving cause for concern. The availability of credit and extended warranty cover facilities were important supplements to the goods on offer for sale.

Pricing

The electrical goods retailing industry exhibits many of the economist's perfect market characteristics. Numerous sellers operating in the confined areas of high streets offer selections of largely homogeneous products. The buying public thus has the opportunity to shop around for the best deal. HSE, like many leading competitors, offers a 'we'll match any competitor's price' guarantee. As one middle manager explained, 'Twenty-five years ago the HSE salesmen were "kings" around here. Our doorstep selling approach of those times brought new consumer goods to a captive audience. There is no longer such a thing as an HSE customer, however. We now have to attract customers anew – every time they buy. This is all about presentation, service and, particularly, price.'

An internal newssheet *Livewire* keeps staff up to date on price and other variations in the market place (staff phone in relevant information as it appears). Further, staff regularly conduct their own 'espionage' forays in their sales territories. Branch managers hold discretion to match any competitive price offer.

Promotion

The location of sales outlets, their overall ambience and internal display modes were seen as important forms of promotion. More overt promotional mediums included local newspapers and window and in-store display areas. Weekly information bulletins from Head Office provided publicity material and instructions on how to implement the material in order to ensure a uniform approach to publicity and the maintenance of the desired HSE image.

Customer service

Branch managers changed the layout of their stores periodically and kept in mind the need to create 'one big cohesive sales unit' where customers could see all parts of the store (and all ranges of goods on offer) from any position therein. While staff agreed that 'you have to "hit" the customer while he is in or he'll leave and buy the same merchandise across the road', nevertheless, they were increasingly aware of the need to be courteous, friendly and professional in order to differentiate the organisation, particularly from some of its bigger, more impersonal, 'cash and carry' type competitors. Branch managers were particularly proud of the service back-up HSE provided ... 'Sales and Service didn't get on at one time. They thought we were pests and we thought they were unhelpful. Things have changed, thank goodness. We are encouraged to get together more – at training sessions and meetings, or just simply during the working day. We're continually in touch and we help each other. They are quick, flexible and efficient and, unlike many of our competitors who rely on outside service organisations, they're *our own*.'

Customer care

Appendix 2.4 shows complaints statistics obtained from HSE's home authority trading standards department. Interpretation of complaints statistics is recognised as being fraught with difficulties. However, the following points in connection with HSE's customer complaints situation are worth making:

1   In general terms complaints against HSE have been falling since 1979 while turnover has remained constant (at least in value terms) and has, since 1982, been generated predominantly in the home authority area.
2   HSE complaint trends compare favourably with general complaint trends of electrical goods.
3   Staff from the local authority confirm that 'HSE now creates much less work for us than used to be the case' and that, 'HSE's central customer relations department is very useful on those occasions when we remain in dispute with branch managers.'
4   Price complaints as a proportion of total complaints have reduced considerably, perhaps as a consequence of the changed product/market strategy. Trading Standards staff regularly commented that 'We used to have problems sorting out rental payments' and (by way of further comment on the effect product/market strategies can have on complaint situations), 'Going even further back we used to have lots of problems over furniture complaints.'
5   Merchantable quality problems remain consistently the biggest source of complaints. HSE staff feel that this problem is not totally within their control because they do not have a sufficiently strong bargaining position with which to enforce change from the manufacturers – costs incurred in improving manufacturers' product quality capabilities would outweigh the benefits, particularly as any improvements would automatically benefit those competitors who share the same manufacturers.

The organisation therefore adopts a 'cure' rather than 'prevention' approach to product quality failure by:

1   Offering extended warranty cover schemes (see Appendix 2.3).
2   Relying on 'sensible' relationships with suppliers to cater for the return, repair or replacement of rogue products (cash refunds remain the exception rather than the rule in faulty product situations).
3   The provision of efficient, courteous and friendly attention to customers with problems.
4   The installation of an improved central consumer care department.
5   The provision of a speedy collection and repair service.
6   Reliance on improving quality standards (many traditional electrical goods do enjoy improving performance records, generally).

Finance

An early problem was due to the Jamesons not wanting to invest further in HSE – or lose control to outside investors.

Finance has remained a constant problem. Despite the sales of a large portfolio of customer rental accounts and the sale of one-third of HSE's branch outlets and the raising of a £2.36m rights issue in 1985, a £10m annual average net debt and attendant interest charges has been wrestled with continually during the period. Profitability has remained elusive and earnings per share/dividend performance have been poor. Appendix 2.5 charts some financial performance indicators since 1979. During this period, too, HSE has survived a major takeover bid by Philips, the electrical giant, and has lived with the rumour of further takeover attempts.

Inside the organisation

The problems facing David Monks and his top team were not only over external developments. The 'new look' HSE required internal changes, too. The major impetus for this change had to come from David and his aides ...

'The old management was OK. George Jameson was a real gentleman but they tended to visit only the "old guard" – staff who they knew well. To the rest of us they were unapproachable, really. Now the new management team seems to get everywhere – they just call and talk to *anybody*. You can give them your honest opinion, too. I wouldn't have dared go against the views of the old management. We've also started bi-monthly meetings (we hire some hotel room) which David Monks chairs. Those are really good for passing information and airing views. You come out of them really buzzing. ...'

'I am impressed with their sharpness of mind. You talk to them and they don't take notes, or anything, but two or three days later you get a memo which directly covers the issues which you raised. I suggested to Mr Sparkes that we could reschedule our 'customers in arrears' visits more efficiently. A couple of days later he wrote to say we'd adopt my ideas. Things are working much better there now. They gave me a small bonus, too.'

'You visit Head Office and you look out for Mr Monks' door. It is almost always open. I could pick up the phone here and now and speak to him directly. Which other major company in this field has such direct links between branch staff and the top man?'

'He gets involved with customers, quite often taking their telephone complaints personally. I'm not sure that the old team knew what customers were. Also we used to have to follow fixed rules but one of the worst things you can do is to quote rules at a complaining customer. Each one needs to be treated separately and, if necessary, uniquely. ...'

'I think we needed somebody to look at things in a cool, professional way. The new management team has done this.'

David Monks is aware of the need to create team spirit ... 'create a good team and the *team* will resolve problems'. His assertion that the new style of management at HSE is 'simply a new post-war Christian approach to management' needs to be viewed, however, in the context of his team's record on the making of tough decisions and the taking of 'hard lines' on certain issues ...

'Basically you've got to tell everyone what is expected of them' and 'We're looking for "sparkle" in this organisation. We are getting there but it hasn't been easy. We've had to work hard at getting people talking to each other and working together. Many suffered culture shock, too, when they were required to sell something other than a Hoover product. We had to train staff to sell a range of different products. Also we had no 25s to 35s in the organisation. All the talent had moved out. We've reintroduced the younger element – largely through internal development and promotions. Just about all the old executive have gone voluntarily. Most were just not up to it, although some had potential and will undoubtedly be better now that they have gained experience of more professional approaches elsewhere.'

Younger, early 30s, managers are now enjoying the positions that might only have been available to them in their late 40s.

'... Also, we had to get people *doing* things. For example, the top executive meetings used to be simply an easy afternoon's "get together". Now I take notes, we agree points of action and use the sessions as springboards for doing things .... At one stage we did get into harmful 'scoring points' games with the unions. In the end we just had to be 'tough skinned' and carry on with our plans.'

A major impetus towards improved organisational performance has been the introduction of a new £400,000 computerised control system. Improvements in credit and stock control have resulted. Information technology has also helped create less overt, but nevertheless real benefits associated with improved staff motivation. Inside the organisation the setting of, and speedy performance feedback on sales targets has fixed organisation attention on the important objectives of increased turnover and profitability ...

'We are involved in what I'd call friendly competition with other branches. We know how well everybody is doing. For example, we are currently third in the league behind Leicester and Buxton. But we've only been open at this site for the past six months. We'll catch them. ...'

'The bonus is useful, of course, but this is the real "turn on". Charting ourselves against targets each week is a great motivator in itself. ...'

'The whole mood of the branch depends upon how Monday's print-outs of the previous week's figures compare with our targets. If they are up, so are we. If they're down we have to shake ourselves out of despondency by discussing why they are down and how we are going to get back on schedule. ...'

Another successful manager, however, commented on some of the more difficult aspects of the system ... 'It's like any business, I suppose. The better you do the better they want you to do. I've done well and so my targets are a lot higher than many of my colleagues. I've got to meet the new targets or my personal earnings will suffer – but there's a limit to the growth. I have eight major competitors within half a mile of this branch. We are still suffering the effects of the miners' strike and the County Council has, of course, just been abolished. The end of council-subsidised bus fares means that travelling costs around here have gone up three or fourfold. People aren't coming into town as much as they used to. The pressure is always on.'

Despite the many changes successfully achieved over the past few years at HSE, conditions, then, remain difficult. David Monks appreciates that the quest for safety and growth is an enduring one and that success is relative – it needs to be measured in terms of the internal and external opportunities and constraints which are major factors in the success equation. He remains cautiously optimistic ... 'We are getting there. The organisation now has "sparkle". Turnover is up 6 per cent on last year despite increased competition. We have achieved breakeven twice (better than the £4m loss situation we inherited). We are shaking off the shackles of our rental policy – and we are, of course, still in work. We must now push on for greater profitability.'

David's hope must be for the realisation of a young, newly promoted manager's enthusiastic claim ... 'I've never been so excited and proud about the job and the organisation. The "new HSE" is where it's at. We're the force in electrical retailing.'

Appendix 2.1 *Typical media extracts on the electrical goods retail trade 1984–86*

(a) A furious row erupted yesterday over the news that the Granada Group has made a conditional agreement to buy the Comet electrical retailing group should Dixons win its unwanted takeover bid for Woolworths. Since its takeover of Rediffusion in 1984, for £120m, Granada TV rental has become the biggest in the TV rental business with 650 high street outlets. Last year it tested the sale of manufacturer branded goods in its Scottish shops and found that one-third of revenue was generated by retail, without significant adverse impact on the rental business. As a result by the end of this year it is planned that two-thirds of Granada's shops will offer TVs for sale and thus double its potential market. Comet is the leading name in the edge of town section operating 60 per cent of the UK outlets in this sector. Woolworths' director, Mr Nigel Whittaker called the offer 'ludicrous' and suggested that if Alex Bernstein at Granada were to get Comet at the price Mr Kalas has suggested he would be 'laughing all the way to the bank'.

(b) HSE the northern electrical goods group and the Leeds chain, Vallances are among the first set of retailers nationally to sell Sir Clive Sinclair's controversial battery powered vehicle, the C5. The vehicle will be on display in some 22 of HSE's stores and test drives are planned in the car parks of the chain's superstores. For HSE, the massive publicity for the C5 is well timed to fit in with its new superstore strategy, and yesterday – the first day when the C5 was put up for sale in HSE outlets – was also the first day of the group's shareholders meeting to approve a £2.36m rights issue, the proceeds of which are to go towards developing superstore sites. David Monks, HSE's managing director described the C5 development as

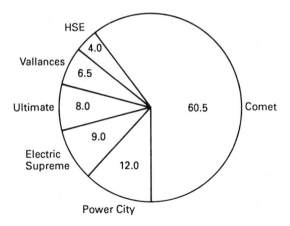

How Comet dominate the out-of-town retailing

'exciting' but would not say how many of the vehicles, which retail at £399 each, were in stock.

(c)   HSE, the white and brown goods retailer, is raising £2.36m fresh capital with a rights issue of 7 per cent convertible preference shares. Managing director, David Monks who arrived at lossmaker HSE from Rumbelows in May 1982, said yesterday the money would be used to implement a five-year plan which would see four superstore, edge of town outlets, open each year while smaller high street sites (HSE has 96 of these) would be updated and closely scrutinised for profitability. The fresh capital will also go towards a computerised sales system. Mr Monks says that, currently some ten days could lapse between sales figures being transmitted, so that outlets ran out of stock.

Patient HSE shareholders must be wondering when HSE will turn around. Yesterday's announcement was accompanied by a gloomy forecast that the year to March would see losses of not more than £75,000. This is against a £35,000 profit last time. HSE put the blame on competitive trading, recent interest rate rises and the continuing miners' strike which, it says, has cost the group £400,000 profit in the current year. No dividend has been paid for the past three years but the board will recommend a 2.5p net for the year to March 1986.

(d)   Telefusion, the Blackpool TV rental and electrical goods retailer, yesterday produced interim results which underline the need for its decision to combine both businesses and rename all its stores Connect. The relaunch of its 200 or more stores in the new colours cost £900,000 up to October, and this, along with a £5m downturn in turnover and severe problems in the high street business before the name change brought about a pre-tax loss of £367,000 against a £1.25m profit last time.

(e)   Dixons, the camera to hi-fi group newly expanded after its bitter Currys takeover coup, yesterday sold something few people realised it had – snuff. Permaflex is a Dixons subsidiary and is the subject of a management buy-out. Eleven months on, the Dixons/Currys operation is widely regarded in the City as the perfect double act. Already market leaders in camera sales, the new 800 store operation will soon be selling one in four of the brown goods sold in the UK. Combined sales and profit are well in excess of the sum of previous individual performance figures. Dixons has recently sold 210,000 TV rental contracts (acquired from Currys). Dixons' view is that selling and renting sets should not be carried out by the same outlets. Dixons' retail policies have translated into useful financial performances. Earnings per share are up from 19.5p in 1982 to 35.8p in 1985. Share prices (annual averages) have moved from £2.08 in 1982 to £7.50 in 1985. Turnover and profits of £117m and £6m respectively grew to £275m and £22m, respectively, over the same period.

(f) The Japanese electronics industry is set to plunge the audio market into another revolutionary phase that threatens to kill off the compact disc market before development costs have been recovered. The newcomer is the digital audio tape (dat). Deliveries of compact disc equipment to trade outlets rose to 147,000 units last year compared with 17,000 in 1983. The total is expected to reach half a million this year. The music industry gives a warning that 'if DAT is allowed to arrive on the market in an untimely and disorderly appearance, it might be the final blow to the recording industry'.

Sales of electronic home entertainment products have dropped by £500,000 in the past two years. The industry is 'currently ploughing a furrow between the crests of product development'. Home computer and video sales have levelled off while the development of products which link with each other will not reach the market before the 1990s. The sectors most likely to grow are television sets, video cameras and in-car entertainment. The home computer market appears to be at saturation point. Sales in the small audio market – radios, recorders and walkmen – peaked in 1984.

Appendix 2.2 *Business Monitor statistics*

Retail sales (£m)

	1980	*1982*	*1984*
Photographic and optical goods	401	464	434
Audio visual equipment hire and relay	962	1125	1182

Appendix 2.3 *HSE proposal form*

| DIS | 115 | Extended Warranty covers new products only and must be applied for within 30 days from the date of purchase as new |

| 2039 | 03 | Title   Initials   Surname |

Name

Address

Postcode

Date of Purchase

Make

Model   Purchase Price £

THE ORIGINAL MANUFACTURER'S GUARANTEE (ONE YEAR UNLESS OTHERWISE STATED) COMMENCING AT DATE OF PURCHASE EXTENDED TO 5 YEARS IN ALL.
(Please place a cross in one box only.)

		Premium			Premium
Monochrome TV	1	☐ £13.49	Audio Equipment and Colour		
Colour TV	2	☐ £37.99	Television up to 20" combined	10	☐ £59.99
Colour TV, 2 year Manufacturers Guarantee	3	☐ £31.99	Twin Tub	11	☐ £38.99
Laser Video	4	☐ £79.99	Tumble Dryer	12	☐ £33.99
Video Disc		☐ £39.99	Freezer or Fridge Freezer	13	☐ £19.99
Digital Audio or Compact Disc	5	☐ £64.99	Freezer or Fridge Freezer with		
Audio Equipment up to £150	6	☐ £23.99	Food Spoilage limit £300	14	☐ £29.99
Audio Equipment £151 to £500	7	☐ £28.99	Refridgerator	15	☐ £17.99
Audio Equipment £501 to £1000	8	☐ £39.99	Microwave Oven up to £300	16	☐ £29.99
Audio Equipment and Colour			Microwave Oven over £300	17	☐ £29.99
Television up to 16" combined	9	☐ £59.99	Vacuum Cleaner	27	☐ £13.99

THE ORIGINAL MANUFACTURER'S ONE YEAR GUARANTEE COMMENCING AT DATE OF PURCHASE EXTENDED TO:-

		3 years in all			5 years in all
Home Computer up to £200 Console only	18	☐ £22.99			
Video Cassette Recorder	19	☐ £49.99		23	☐ £97.99
Automatic Washing Machine	20	☐ £39.99		24	☐ £89.99
Automatic Washer Dryer	21	☐ £49.99		25	☐ £119.99
Dishwasher	22	☐ £34.99		26	☐ £79.99

FOR DEALER USE	Please hand to shop staff who will issue you with a receipt or forward to H.S.E. "Supercover" Department, together with a copy of your sale receipt as proof of purchase. Cheques should be made payable to:
Branch code	
Cost centre	
Staff No.	

Branch Name   Tog   Man   Model

5 | 4

N.B. the premiums shown for the periods of cover indicated apply until the 28th February 1986.

Credit Account Number   Cash Transaction

Appendix 2.4 *Electrical goods and consumer complaints statistics*

HSE Ltd : Annual complaints level (volume)

1979	1980	1981	1982	1983	1984
808	700	702	609	544	548

Source: Home Authority records of complaints registered at Consumer Advice centres

Industry complaint totals

1981	1982	1983	1984
3,956	4,300	5,105	5,027

Source: Home Authority records of complaints registered at Consumer Advice centres

Appendix 2.5 *HSE financial performance indicators*

Year	t/o	Pre-tax profit £ millions	Earnings per share	Gross dividend	Share price	
1979	41.9	1.85	20p	2.5p	–	
1980	44.3	0.91	14.9p	1.1p	–	
1981	45.3	0.63	9.6p	1.6p	–	
1982	42.4	–3.72	–71.5p	Nil	98p	(lowest)
1983	40.6	–1.68	–18.8p	Nil	2.00	(highest)
1984	41.2	–0.05	0.7p	Nil	1.30	(average)
1985	46.3	+0.035	–1.2p	Nil	1.15	(lowest)
1986	55.0	+0.355	0.7p	2.5p	1.30	(average)

Extract from Chairman's statement year ended 1986:
'Price inflation in our sector remains low and total spending on electrical products increased by 9 per cent on last year. Against this background our retail turnover performance has been commendable.'

HSE Ltd – balance sheets

	1981 £000	1982 £000	1985 £000	1986 £000
Fixed assets	25,468	23,790	17,063	14,034
Current assets				
Stocks	Not	Not	7395	7834
Debtors	avail	avail	6442	6451
Cash	able	able	118	142
	13,765	10,140	13,955	14,427
Current liabilities				
Creditors falling due within one year	(17,078)	(15,100)	(12,769)	(12,129)
Net current assets	(3,313)	(4,960)	1,186	2,298
Total assets *less* current liabilities	22,155	18,830	18,249	16,332
Creditors due after more than one year	7,173	7,569	(5,421)	(3,366)
Deferred taxation			(75)	(75)
Net assets	14,982	11,261	12,753	12,891
Capital and reserves				
Called up share capital	1316	1316	3918	3918
Reserves	13666	9945	8835	8973
	14,982	11,261	12,753	12,891

26 Retailing

HSE Ltd – consolidated profit and loss account for the year ended 29 March 1986

	1986 £000	1985 £000
Turnover	55,003	46,308
Cost of sales	(49,488)	(41,499)
Gross profit	5,515	4,809
Operating costs	(4,057)	(3,546)
Interest payable	(1,103)	(1,325)
Profit/(loss) on ordinary activities before taxation	355	(62)
Taxation	(133)	–
Profit/(loss) on ordinary activities after taxation	222	(62)
Extraordinary items	65	(100)
Profit/(loss) for the financial year	287	(162)
Dividends	(318)	(1)
Transfer from reserves	(31)	(163)
Earnings per ordinary share	0.7p	−1.2p

3 · What Next?

Bill Richardson

In the space of five short but increasingly hectic years of self-generated change, during the early 1980s, Next plc changed the fortunes of its founding parent company and the face of British fashion retailing. A look at its developments and some of the forces and philosophies behind them seemed, inevitably, to stimulate the question 'What Next?' What did come next took many people by surprise.

Some organisational developments

1981 • J Hepworth Ltd, the menswear manufacturer and retailer, appoints George Davies to lead the development of a chain of women's fashionwear shops.

1982 • With Davies as managing director, Next plc begins trading.

1984 • Next for Men chain is launched.
• Hepworth computer services begins a three-year project using IBM point of sale terminals in the Next outlets to improve and integrate purchase order management, stock distribution and replenishment, sales collation, financial planning and forecasting.

1985 • Next Interior launched.
• Hepworth becomes subsumed by Next.
• Leeds Head Office is relocated in Leicestershire.
• Total ownership is taken of Club 24 (formerly run with Forward Trust). Club 24 provides credit facilities for Next customers and for the customers of other stores such as Dixons, Mothercare and Etam.

1986 • Next franchises opened in Norway, Cyprus, Qatar and Antwerp.
• Paul James Knitwear manufacturer is bought.
• Grattan, the number four British mail order organisation, is bought for £300m.
• Next Collection, aimed more specifically at Next's working women customers, and Next Too, directed at existing customer bases but concentrating on more casual garments, are launched.

1987 • A programme of bigger 'Complete Next', city centre stores development begins.

- £338m buys Combined English Stores, the Zales to Salisbury retailer. Next's bid is accepted in the face of competition from Gerald Ratner of the newly successful Ratners plc, and from Etam plc. The purchase provides an extra 700,000 square footage of selling space (increasing existing Next space by 80 per cent) and takes the pressure off Next's planned 400,000 square foot per year growth programme.
- Fil a Fil, a retailer of men's and women's fashions is bought for £800,000. Its chain of 400 to 500 square foot retail premises are to be used as additional outlets for Next's shoes and accessories shops.
- £3m is paid for a 51 per cent interest in Van Overdijk, a Belgian suitmaker. Next considers itself an informed investment partner working with, rather than controlling the existing management.
- 50 per cent interest in the Paige Group is acquired from Great Universal Stores which receives 4.5 million Next shares (a 1.27 per cent stake in return). Paige offers a 197 strong chain of women's wear shops doing little more than breaking even.
- Dillons, a 270 outlet chain of newsagents, is bought in connection with Next's 'revolutionary plans for its mail order business'. Next plans are said to include two-day mail order responses to telephone orders and newsagency collection points. This acquisition is greeted with some scepticism by business commentators.
- Sixteen Next BG (Boys and Girls) stores are opened. Six of these are autonomous, the others forming independent sections in Next grown up shops. Forty such outlets are intended by the end of the year.

George Davies

Any study of Next quickly reveals that it is almost impossible to separate the systems, structures and strategies of the organisation from its managing director (and newly incumbent chairman) George Davies, whose philosophies and ideas are reflected within the organisation in a wide variety of ways. Born in Liverpool in 1942, the son of a sausage and pie production manager father and a Post Office worker mother, George Davies went on to attend Bootle Grammar School and Birmingham University. He threw in his dentistry studies in 1960 after getting the bug for retailing from holiday jobs at Littlewoods. His first full-time job (with Littlewoods) was followed in 1970 by his own children's wear mail order venture (which ultimately failed). In 1974, following the demise of the business, Davies joined Pippa Dee, the party plan home sales fashion company. A successful era with this organisation ended, however, in 1981 after a boardroom row following a takeover battle. Within a matter of days, his contacts in the industry had put him in touch with Hepworth, the UK's second biggest menswear manufacturer/retailer. Struggling to come to terms with a situation which had seen UK sales of men's suits fall during the

1970s from volumes of 10 million to 4 million, Hepworth, via its chairman, Terence Conran, appointed Davies. His immediate task was to take Hepworth, via women's fashion, into the new retailing era of the 1980s. His retail background provided Hepworth with, to use Davies' own words 'a broadly based business guy who sees keeping in touch with the customer as vital'.

Davies is definitely a 'hands on' manager who involves himself in all areas of product market operations and in the range of functional activities. He has the capacity to take on and contribute to the range of business operations from warehousing to computer systems design and continues to take the lead in thinking up and implementing new strategic ideas. Total commitment to Next, and an obvious enjoyment of his job, sees him spending Saturday evenings at home with wife Elizabeth (production director of Next) attaining 'a big turn on still' from checking out trading results for the week via his portable computer. Last year's Mauritius holiday produced little in the way of a suntan but more in the form of an acquired garment manufacturer. 'He spent all day, every day, in the factory', Elizabeth says. Davies kits himself out, almost entirely, in Next clothes.

Above all, perhaps, Davies is an 'ideas man' and a quick learner. While Terence Conran reminds us that Davies was not the only person behind the Hepworth to Next transformation – 'I'm tired of hearing that George Davies reinvented the high street. It was Conran Design Group which designed the stores and John Stephenson who now works at Storehouse who came up with the name. Now all we hear is young George getting all the credit.' Davies has, nevertheless, undoubtedly been in the driving seat for the development of the Next concept. While Davies freely admits that the original concept was not so well-formulated as it appears to have been with hindsight, he reminds us that 'we quickly realised that we had something really special going for us.' The success with which he has refined and developed the concept and associated Next operations won him the Guardian Young Businessman Award for 1985.

Colleagues refer to Davies not only as an exceptional ideas man but also one who creates the sort of atmosphere in which people want to work. Analysts regard him highly referring to his effective management style (*everyone* calls him George), his high reputation and his ability to build a team which has, according to some commentators, 'people in the lower levels who are capable of meeting the high standards he sets'. Personnel and associates are also aware that underneath the open door management style is a tough operator capable of single-minded dogmatism over his Next ideas and plans.

Davies considers himself, above all, to be a man of integrity. Once his word is given a contract is not necessary. Certainly he is loyal. Many of those who supported him during the final period of his time at Pippa Dee are now with him at Next.

Market segmentation

At the heart of the Next success story is the ability to find (or create) financially attractive market gaps and to exploit them to the full. Early, less defined, segmentation aspirations were to sell clothes to the more affluent working women who 'had outgrown Chelsea Girl but didn't want to shop in Marks & Spencer'. Today, segmentation skills and perceptions are more sophisticated and related more clearly to the Next mission. Davies claims, 'We like to do things in a certain way – whatever we do. It is a mission.' The mission reflects Davies' own view of how Next should be perceived – 'Visionary, different, well-designed and functional, and satisfying a customer need for exclusivity'. The approach underlying Next activity extends to the impressive village-Head Office in the Leicester countryside which has been nominated for a special design award. Davies sees his expression of mission permeating the total organisation.

The 'exclusivity' fundamental, however, brings problems to Davies' continuing hunger for growth. Growth and exclusivity do not go hand in hand. Furthermore, existing market players such as Marks & Spencer and newer entrants such as Benetton have all tried to emulate Next's success formulae and to attract growing shares of Next's 'Yuppie-ish' market. Faced with these twin problems, the Next solution appears to revolve around two strategies. On the one hand, growth is being achieved by moves into new areas of business rather than through attempting to create mass markets from existing customer bases. In Davies' words, 'We have moved into different markets so we haven't hit the problems that occur when you go for massive volumes in one market.' On the other hand, the organisation is further segmenting its existing markets. Next itself has recently (1987) been sub-segmented into Next Collection, offering clothes for the traditional Next customer who is primarily looking for stylish workwear and into Next Too, aimed at the Next customer when she is seeking a more casual, less constrained wardrobe.

Ultimately, of course, continuous sub-segmentation ends in a situation where *every* customer is perceived as a market segment – a scenario which will depend upon the ability of store staff to respond to their customers in a very personal manner.

The marketing mix

'At the end of the day, it is about product', says Davies. 'Unless the product is regarded as the central issue in retailing, then retailers having problems will not solve them.' Product attractiveness and basic quality is, of course, essential if the reality of a Next purchase is to meet the customer's expectations.

Product failure destroys the potential effectiveness of other aspects of the marketing mix. 'Unless the products are altered to become attractive, frequent interior design changes are necessary to keep the customers.' Given this basic perception of the importance of product, it is not surprising that the Next organisation works closely with its manufacturers and rather than buying in manufacturer's creations, takes responsibility itself for designing the clothes that are expected to prove attractive to next year's customer. Once again, the offer of exclusivity produces problems. Next store staff expect – and deal with

– the hassle of customers complaining that lack of availability of garments 'similar to my friend's' is due to organisational inefficiency.

Exclusivity and product quality, however, do attract value-adding price premiums. Next's pricing policies have, reputedly, been deliberately set at Marks & Spencer type prices, plus at least 10 per cent.

Selling staff are instructed that 'Next is about personal service. Self-service is what you get at supermarkets.' The Next Selling Skills package is supplemented by 12 weeks' training for Next's 'Sales Consultants'. Body language secrets and those of the best way to approach customers are features of training programmes.

Retailing revolves, to some large extent, on how property developers see the value of a site. The strength of sites held by Hepworth and Burtons helped both organisations through the leaner years of the late 1970s and early 1980s. The newly enlarged portfolio of properties enables Next senior management to play the chessboard of rearranging the total Next chain location structure. The portfolio is flexible. Market research determines which sites are most suitable for particular categories of Next type customers. For example, if Salisbury is expected to do better in Burton-on-Trent than the existing Next for Men store, then Salisbury will move in and Next for Men will move out. Twelve 'Complete' stores (offering around 25,000 to 40,000 square feet of selling space) were in operation by 1987. These were lighter and bigger than the traditional Next outlets. All offer an uncluttered purchase situation. Effective stock replacement systems facilitate this approach. Staff are encouraged to take pride in their stores – the high street presence of Next is regarded as the major potential generator of sales. Window displays are designed and changed by a mobile team directed by Head Office although the creative flair of the store staff is put to good use on the internal display areas, giving each site its own subtle personality. The total ambience of the Next purchase experience is intended to provide a marked differentiation from that provided by their 'market trader type', mass market competitors.

Next postcards and diaries, splashed with currently in vogue Next colours, supplement ads placed in well-chosen magazines. Davies, himself, tends to rely on the promotional creativity within Next rather than on that supplied by advertising agencies. Advised to allocate £1m for the initial promotion of Next, he instituted a successful campaign which cost just £80,000. In totality, then, the Next marketing mix aims to achieve what Davies describes as the essence of retailing – creating the right illusions for the customer. The Next purchase experience seems, to date, to have successfully bridged the gap between satisfying the functional clothing requirements of customers and providing a purchase experience which enables customers to express their own preferred self identities.

Inside the Organisation

Davies' own strong philosophies have, not unnaturally, been major influencers in shaping the culture of the organisation. One appropriate maxim for the organisational approach to strategic development seems to be 'Ready, Fire, Aim'. In fact, much thought and evaluation goes into developments underlying the constant change which Davies sees as fundamental to continuing success. 'Because we keep developing, we keep changing, and that helps keep the image fresh. The only way forward is to change. But as captives of their own industry most organisations resist change. They defend their one goal lead. They only change when they are going broke, when they are 5–0 down. We mustn't defend Next. There's no sacred cow about Next.' Operationally, of course, such philosophies mean that store fitters, for example, find working to tight deadlines an essential part of their jobs, and middle management is required to demonstrate practically Davies' commendations of strength in depth and capability to handle massive, dynamic growth.

New ways of thinking about the retail industry are encouraged. In order to offer the newly targeted 'Juppies' (junior urban professionals) special attention and new ideas, for example, the organisation has brought in designers who *don't* usually design for children. Next has also avoided manufacturers which specialise in children's fabrics in a bid to develop new products and update the image of children's clothing. Concern over this type of approach has, however, been expressed in the context of the organisation's move into jewellery and its 'kicking out' of Combined English Store's jewellery industry experts – despite Next's own lack of in-house expertise in this area. Next might defend itself against such allegations by referring to its track record as a *retailer* – regardless of the goods and/or services being offered. Its retailing mission comes through in George Davies' comments on the move further into the financial services industry... 'Most retailers have moved into financial services through the prompting of their accountancy arms. We are doing it as retailers and will treat them like other products we market in the high street.'

'Closeness to the customer' provides another organisational maxim. In the new children's venture, for example, the emphasis is on understanding the child – not the mother. Next understand that today's kids know their own minds. A range is being created for 12 years old *down* rather than from maternity up, like Mothercare. 'Inside' the organisation, too, includes suppliers... 'We've worked and worked at our supply system. We had to find suppliers who think, like us, of the final customer. We are both in it together. It's a very fine balance between buyer and supplier and we can't be dominant.'

Provided personnel operate within the core constraints of putting the company and the customer first, then an aura of informality prevails. Managers and staff talk and *listen* to each other. Head Office provides one canteen, no boardroom and few rules.

Finance

Commercial organisations are judged ultimately on financial performance. On this front Next, once again, shows up well. Its very ambitious programme of development has so far worked successfully. In the five years to 1986, sales have doubled to just under £200m and profits have leapt sevenfold. Investors buying into the company ten years ago will have seen their money increase by around 40 times. Until the more recent heavy acquisition programme the gearing, too, has always been conservative. A £100m rights issue has paid for the 1986/87 developments and put the organisation into a useful position for progressing into the future. Appendix 3.1 provides more detailed financial performance information.

Future developments

Needless to say, Next has no intention of resting on its laurels. Future developments which seem likely to be pursued include:

- Moves via agency/franchise arrangements (with Gary Weston of Associated British Foods – with whom George Davies 'gets on very well') into the United States and Canada.
- Development into the under-25 fashion market – and the inevitable clashes with giants, Burtons and Sears.
- 'Next Gentlemen' and 'Next Ladies' as the organisation seeks to retain its customers as they grow up.
- The progression of Club 24 to 'licensed deposit-taker' status and into mortgage and insurance business.
- A highly innovatory approach to mail order business.

One thing seems certain for all those associated with Next. A sure answer to the question of 'What Next?' is 'Change – and more change!' (See Appendix 3.5 for an indication of the changes which occurred.)

34 Retailing

Appendix 3.1 *Next plc – financial information*

Consolidated profit and loss account (£000)

	Aug 31 1982	Aug 31 1983	Aug 31 1984	Aug 31 1985	Aug 31 1986
Turnover	83,370	98,603	108,331	146,045	190,021
Cost of sales	73,387	85,542	90,494	119,322	152,984
Gross profit	9,983	13,061	17,837	26,723	37,037
Distribution costs	2,361	2,308	2,746	3,437	5,524
Administrative expenses	5,018	5,405	5,902	7,273	9,750
Associated company's loss	–	–	–	–	294
Non-consolidated subsidiary's profit	(3,644)	(3,926)	(4,475)	(4,740)	(7,044)
Interest	2,388	713	48	690	854
Profit (loss) before tax	3,860	8,561	13,616	20,063	27,659
Corporation tax	–	2,229	5,256	5,833	6,770
Deferred tax	–	54	1,087	2,319	1,060
Overseas tax	–	49	62	85	109
Non-consolidated subsidiary's tax	92	91	113	116	2,648
Prior year tax	(209)	(288)	(1,087)	(82)	(813)
Total taxation	(117)	2,135	5,431	8,271	9,744
Profit (loss) after tax	3,977	6,426	8,185	11,792	17,885
Preference dividends	64	64	64	64	64
Profit after preference dividends	3,913	6,362	8,121	11,728	17,821
Ordinary dividends	1,751	2,438	3,449	5,053	11,460
Extraordinary items	(1,529)	(808)	(461)	(2,147)	563
Retained profit (loss)	3,691	4,732	5,133	8,822	5,798
Holding company	3,363	1,541	2,074	3,127	(10,782)
Subsidiaries	328	3,191	3,059	5,695	16,874
Associated companies	–	–	–	–	(294)
Retained profit (loss)	3,691	4,732	5,133	8,822	5,798
Interest					
Bank loans and overdrafts	1,559	877	199	729	1,545
Medium-term loan	1,020	–	–	67	–
Debentures					
Within 5 Years	–	15	8	–	33
After 5 Years	102	75	73	73	40
Capitalised	–	–	–	–	(409)
	2,681	967	280	869	1,209
Receivable	(293)	(254)	(232)	(179)	(355)
	2,388	713	48	690	854

	Aug 31 1982	Aug 31 1983	Aug 31 1984	Aug 31 1985	Aug 31 1986
Profit before tax is after charging/(crediting)					
Depreciation					
Leasehold property	329	342	391	287	
Plant and vehicles	626	701	850	1,238	5,719
Retail plant and fittings	1,922	2,019	2,382	2,522	
Operating lease rentals					
Plant and machinery	554	620	623	373	563
Other	–	–	4,269	8,190	11,774
Property repairs and					
maintenance	438	–	–	–	–
Auditors' remuneration	67	57	69	72	
Directors'					
Emoluments	257	300	340	329	559
Compensation	–	–	–	–	100
Staff costs					
Wages and salaries	16,429	16,833	17,288	20,874	27,488
Social security	1,836	1,590	1,581	1,810	2,076
Pension	450	425	342	327	551
Share scheme	20	20	74	182	237
	18,735	18,868	19,285	23,193	30,352
Average number of					
employees	4,057	3,858	3,462	4,493	8,193
Corporation tax rate %	–	52	47.9	42.9	37.9
Extraordinary items					
Properties realisation	(2,806)	(1,906)	(1,319)	(4,712)	(1,233)
Closure and costs	1,385	1,203	762	4,524	3,019
Interest disposal	–	379	311	–	–
Deferred tax	–	–	(2,312)	–	–
Trans from reserves	–	–	2,312	–	–
Debenture redemption	(108)	–	–	–	–
	(1,529)	(324)	(246)	(188)	1,786
Taxation	–	(484)	(215)	(1,959)	(1,223)
	(1,529)	(808)	(416)	(2,147)	563

1987 (May) rankings of UK Companies by market capitalisation

Rank	Company	Price (p)	Value (m)
103	Royal Bank of Scotland	324	921.1
104	Unigate	398	895.9
105	Next	343	873.8
106	Burmah Oil	502	867.3
107	RMC Group	887	844.4

Appendix 3.2 *Next plc – organisation activities – to November 1986*

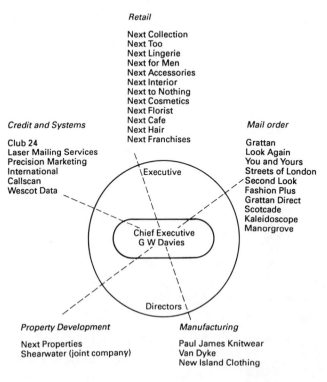

Next Group Activities 1986

Retail

Next Collection
Next Too
Next Lingerie
Next for Men
Next Accessories
Next Interior
Next to Nothing
Next Cosmetics
Next Florist
Next Cafe
Next Hair
Next Franchises

Credit and Systems

Club 24
Laser Mailing Services
Precision Marketing
International
Callscan
Wescot Data

Mail order

Grattan
Look Again
You and Yours
Streets of London
Second Look
Fashion Plus
Grattan Direct
Scotcade
Kaleidoscope
Manorgrove

Executive

Chief Executive
G W Davies

Directors

Property Development

Next Properties
Shearwater (joint company)

Manufacturing

Paul James Knitwear
Van Dyke
New Island Clothing

Retail outlet by activity	Aug. 85	Aug. 86	Nov. 86	1987
Next Too		112	117	
Next Collection	210	109	114	
Next for Men	114	162	174	
Next Lingerie	0	5	42	
Next Accessories (stand alone)	0	3	8	
Next Interior	14	36	40	
Next Cafe	5	9	10	
Next Espresso Bar	1	6	8	
Next Florist	5	8	8	
Next Hairdressers	0	3	3	
Next to Nothing	2	15	23	
Hepworth	84	0	0	
	435	468	547	

More recent additions:
– Salisbury   150
– Zales/Collingwood/Weir   265
– Paige   208

Appendix 3.3 *Next plc – some market sector information*

(a) *Mail order*
Sales rose to £3bn in 1986 after a recession in the early 1980s. This represents
6 per cent of total retail spending. Some forecasters reckon sales in this sector
will achieve £4.5bn by 1990. Younger, middle-class customers are beginning to
show interest in this form of non-shop shopping, although the dominant
customer base remains the older, lower-class segment. 1986 mail order market
shares included:

GUS	42.0%
Littlewoods	25.3%
Freemans	13.7%
Grattan	10.2%
Empire	6.2%
Other	2.6%

Source: Verdict Research

(b) *Newsagency industry*
The market for newsagent's shops remains buoyant. Four of the UK's seven
largest newsagent chains have changed hands during 1986/87. This bid activity
reflects to some extent the fact that newsagents are about the last retailing
business to resist conglomeration. Independents still dominate – even the
largest operator, W H Smith, only accounts for about 7 per cent of the UK's
£8bn annual expenditure on confectionery, tobacco and newspapers. The small
man – helped by his family – can still run a shop in a way that bigger chains
would find uneconomical. Also the near monopoly of newspaper distribution
enjoyed by wholesalers means that new entrants have to buy an existing
newsagent, as the wholesalers are reluctant to supply new outlets.

However, while the price of existing newsagent outlets seems set to maintain
at least at existing levels the profitability of the industry will remain unexciting.
With two-thirds of newsagency sales derived from newspapers and tobacco the
industry suffers from declining market demand for both products. Further, the
newsagent cannot compete through the exercise of purchase muscle power as
can its supermarket competitors in the confectionery market.

(c) *Children's clothing*
With the children of the 1960s' baby boom now themselves beginning to breed,
forecasters are anticipating the growth of the importance of the pre-teen market.
In 1986 the children's clothing market was worth £2.2bn. Market shares were
estimated as being:

Marks & Spencer	11.0%
Mothercare (strong in babywear)	9.0%
British Home Stores	4.5%
Woolworths	3.5%
Boots	3.0%

Industry players are preparing themselves to take their shares of the growing market. Boots is to spend £100m on its Children's World venture, Woolworths plans to open 100 kids' stores over the next five years.

The new 'Yuppie' generation seems certain to have the freedom to pick and choose.

Appendix 3.4 *The price and yields of prime retail space – 1987*

Shop rents		£ per annum	Shop investment yields		%
1	New York	297,000	1	Switzerland	3.5
2	Zurich	258,000	2	UK	4.0
3	Geneva	228,000	3	West Germany	5.0
4	London	200,000	4	Australia	6.0
5	Paris	159,500	5	Holland	7.0
6	San Francisco	148,500	5	Italy	7.0
7	Melbourne	137,500	5	Sweden	7.0
8	Brisbane	118,500	5	USA	7.0
9	Sydney	100,000	6	Belgium	7.5
9	Glasgow	100,000	6	France	7.5

(Based on a 1,500 sq ft prime retail unit – city centre)

(Initial purchasing yields on prime retail properties)

Notes: 1 More than 2.2 million people were employed in the 800m square feet of retail property in Britain in 1987.
2 Annual retail sales value stood at more than £80bn per year.
3 Prime office buildings remain the major attractors of property investment. Shop properties had, however, moved into second place (from under a fifth in the early 1980s to well over a third of total property investment by 1987).
4 61m square feet of out-of-town retail schemes had been put before planners by the end of 1986.

Source: Hillier Parker International Property Bulletin, 1987

Appendix 3.5 *Next in the early 1990s*

The chief executive of Next, Mr David Jones, yesterday (10 April 1991) firmly dismissed rumours that he might be leaving the company following the sale of its Grattan mail order side ... 'I'm staying – and always have been. Someone has read my horoscope and got it wrong.'

Mr Jones was reporting on the year to the end of January in which Next lost £40.7m on its ordinary activities. This included an above-the-line provision of £33.5m against the value of Club 24, the credit card operation which is in the process of being wound up. But the pre-tax loss on ordinary trading is not the end of the story.

As Next reshapes itself for the future it has had to make heavy write-offs and in total there are extraordinary provisions of £170m. These include £77.4m incurred on the sale of Grattan and £50m provision against potential property development losses. The final result is a loss of £222.8m for the year, against the previous year's £10.4m profit. Neither figure is acceptable for a business which last year had sales of £878m and the year before sales topping the £1bn mark.

Following the £165m Grattan sale, Next will have £137m in the bank. But it likely to need every penny of that for the repayment of the two convertible stocks which fall due next year. One of the repayments of £63m is due on 15 January and the other of £125m is due on 14 October next year.

The figures came as no shock to the market, although the shares did slip a penny to 26p. The extraordinary provisions were mostly as expected. But one that had not been foreseen was a £17.5m provision against the stake in BSkyB, the satellite station. The stake is now down to less than 1 per cent. Next has a loan outstanding to BSkyB of £15.5m plus £2.3m in equity, 'If it is successful we will have the money repaid in a couple of years', Mr Jones said.

Mr Jones defended the sale of the Grattan mail order business.'Some people think we have sold the family silver. But mail order is going through a difficult time. ... If we had not done the Grattan deal the company would be tottering on the brink.' He said current trading showed a marginal increase over last year, but last month's increase in VAT had brought added pressure, reducing expectations in the short term. As expected, shareholders do not get a final dividend. Last year the payout was 2p.

On a like-for-like basis Next sales were slightly down on 3 per cent less space and 20 per cent less stock. 'We have a significant number of very good sites and we are reducing a number of sites', said Mr Jones. 'The business is solid. What we've got to do is continue to improve the product. ... We are doing that on ladies' wear, but in menswear we have still got a long way to go.'

For Jones, at the helm of the Next organisation since the Christmas 1988 sacking of George and Liz Davies, the job of recreating Next's 1980s success era remains an immensely difficult one.

Section 2 · Transport

4 · Sealine Ferries Ltd

Gillian Fearn

One of the greatest changes in the latter half of the twentieth century has been the growth of the holiday industry. There has been a particular increase in the number of people taking holidays abroad, either on air package tours or travelling by car and crossing the English Channel by car ferry. French resorts in Brittany are especially popular as destinations for families with young children going on camping holidays or staying at *gites*. Day trips have become popular with Christmas shoppers who travel by the ferries to do their Christmas shopping at duty-free prices in the Normandy supermarkets.

Sealine Ferries Ltd is one of three cross-channel ferry companies (the other two being British Ferries and Townsend-Thoresen) operating the routes Dover–Calais, Dover–Boulogne and, until 1984, Newhaven–Dieppe. Sealine was formerly part of British Rail, but following Government pressure by the Conservative administration, was privatised in 1984. (Both British Ferries and Townsend-Thoresen are now (1991) part of P & O European Ferries.)

The management of Sealine Ferries considers that the company has been reasonably successful in the last ten years or so, in spite of changes in the economic cycle, industrial relations disputes and competition from rival firms. The numbers of summer passengers carried during the period 1978–88 (June–September inclusive) is shown in Appendix 4.1, together with figures for fares and advertising expenditure over the same period. Department of Transport statistics for the industry are shown in Appendix 4.2. The next ten years are likely to pose very different problems.

During the early 1980s there was fierce competition between the ferry companies with a price war which raged until heavy losses by all companies forced them to abandon it at the end of 1982. If one company announced special offers or price cuts, so did all the others.

Almost every year has been marred by industrial relations problems involving either the British or French seamen's unions. Strikes were often timed to coincide with the peak weekends of holiday periods and thousands of British tourists, often with carloads of tired children, were left stranded on docksides. Although most of these disputes were common to all the ferry companies, Sealine fared particularly badly in 1982, 1984 and 1988.

Sealine has constantly attempted to improve its service to passengers and has upgraded its ferries to modern standards of comfort and safety. Its efforts were rewarded in 1987 when the *Travel Trade Gazette* awarded Sealine its

Silver Globe Award for best ferry operator of the year, and in 1988 Sealine won the Car Ferry of the Year award. Safety has always been a high priority of the company, particularly since 1987 when the Zeebrugge disaster shook the whole of the ferry industry: one Friday night in March the Townsend-Thoresen vessel, *Herald of Free Enterprise* sank just outside Zeebrugge harbour after the bow doors had inadvertently been left open. Two hundred people tragically lost their lives.

By 1985, all of the cross-channel ferry companies' fears regarding the threat of a Channel Tunnel began to be realised. There had been several previous attempts to construct a tunnel linking England and France, but all had been abandoned. This time the Prime Minister, Mrs Margaret Thatcher, expressed a personal interest in the project, and it began to look as if it might go ahead. The British and French governments invited companies to submit proposals and on 29 July 1987, Eurotunnel won the concession to build and operate a rail tunnel between Folkestone and Coquelles near Calais. The tunnel would be designed to carry rail passenger and freight traffic and would also operate with a regular service of shuttle trains to carry cars, coaches and lorries and would commence operations in May 1993. It was made clear from the start that the project would be financed entirely by the private sector and that there would be no subsidies from either the British or French governments. This led to considerable uncertainty as to whether the requisite finance could be raised. The project went through a number of financial crises and near abandonments as tunnel costs escalated from the original estimate of £4.87bn to £7.2bn in 1990 (See Appendix 4.3). Sufficient finance to complete the project was finally raised in autumn 1990 and the English and French pilot tunnels met on a historic day in September 1990. The final uncertainty regarding the tunnel's future now seems to have gone.

British Rail has estimated that the Channel Tunnel, together with high speed rail links from London and Paris, will cut the travelling time between the two capitals from over 7 hours (using the current rail/ferry system) to just under 3 hours. Estimates of the future market size and of the Channel Tunnel's future market share vary widely, but it is clear that it will pose a major threat to the cross-channel ferries, particularly those on the Dover–Calais route.

Against this background, the management at Sealine are concerned about the future of their company and how they can compete in a changing environment.

Appendix 4.1 (a) *Sealine Ferries: summer passengers*

	1978	1979	1980	1981	1982	1983	1984	1985	1986	1987	1988
Number of passengers (to the nearest 10,000)	41	25	21	33	49	68	72	56	52	60	63

Appendix 4.1 (b) *Sealine summer ferry fare and comparable route Hoverloyd summer fare (for small car, 2 adults and 2 children)*

	1978	1979	1980	1981	1982	1983	1984	1985	1986	1987
Sealine Ferry fare (£)	50	65	77	72	72	75	70	72	92	96
Hoverloyd fare (£)	80	80	85	88	90	90	95	102	108	113

Appendix 4.1 (c) *Sealine advertising expenditure (£10,000s)*

	1978	1979	1980	1981	1982	1983	1984	1985	1986	1987	1988
Advertising expenditure	8	10	10	15	16	21	25	20	20	30	31

Appendix 4.2 *Department of Transport statistics 1978–88: roll on/roll off ferry traffic*

a) *Road goods vehicles outward → mainland Europe (000s)*

Country of origin	1978	1979	1980	1981	1982	1983	1984	1985	1986	1987	1988
UK	162	179	177	174	181	186	183	180	201	236	255
France	42	53	45	55	66	71	97	96	105	90	107

b) *Accompanied passenger vehicles arrivals and departures → France (000s vehicles)*

	1978	1979	1980	1981	1982	1983	1984	1985	1986	1987	1988
Cars	1043	1075	1204	1402	1531	1489	1484	1589	1944	2020	2020
Coaches	37	40	50	78	95	117	116	118	126	125	119
Hovercraft services	296	374	337	287	231	206	204	208	218	238	262

Appendix 4.3 *Troubled saga of a hole in the ground*

The Channel tunnel has gone from one crisis to the next in the four years since Eurotunnel was selected to build and operate the twin-rail link. A succession of management and financial squabbles and continuing delays in construction have brought the tunnel to the brink of collapse several times.

The Government has been prevented from bailing out the project because the Channel Tunnel Act prohibits public funding. This has left Eurotunnel dependent on the good will of its bankers and the support of private investors. The development of the Eurotunnel project is outlined below:

Jan. 1986:   Eurotunnel wins concession to build the tunnel.

Oct. 1986:   Share issue to raise £206m scrapes home.

Feb. 1987:   Lord Pennock resigns as Eurotunnel chairman and is replaced by Alastair Morton.

April 1987:   Eurotunnel postpones £750m share issue.

June 1987:   Banks agree stop-gap funding of £72.5m.

Aug. 1987:   Eurotunnel gets approval for £5bn loan from worldwide syndicate of 206 banks.

July 1987:   Anglo–French Channel Tunnel Treaty ratified.

Sept. 1987:   Row breaks out between Eurotunnel and Transmanche Link (TML) over escalating costs of the project.

Nov. 1987:   Share issue to raise £770m scrapes home and tunnel costs forecast at £4.87bn.

Aug. 1988:   Eurotunnel dispute with TML over costs worsens.

Oct. 1988:   Cost estimate raised to £5.22bn.

Jan. 1989:   Eurotunnel and TML reach accord. New management brought into TML.

April 1989:   Cost estimate raised to £5.48bn. Opening date put back one month to June 1993.

July 1989:   Cost forecasts rise again to £5.7bn. Eurotunnel confirms it is in default of £5bn credit agreement with banks.

Oct. 1989:   Cost estimate rises to at least £7bn. Eurotunnel seeks new financing.

Jan. 1990:   Cost forecast put at £7.2bn. Eurotunnel receives stop-gap funding of £350m–£400m to prevent financial collapse.

Nearly £2bn has now been spent on the 50-kilometre tunnel. It is one-third built and 50 per cent over the original budget with 3½ years to run before it opens.

5 · Silver Wheels Ltd

Bill Richardson and John Patterson

Scene 1

Silver Wheels Ltd is a small, family-owned coach travel business. Founded at the turn of the century by the present owners' grandparents the concern had grown from a horse and cart operation to a 32-bus operation by 1953 when it became incorporated as a limited company.

In 1984, however, the trading situation was giving one of the directors, George Allen, cause for concern. 'The trouble is', said George, who had called a directors' meeting, 'our trading environment has changed without us really noticing it. Just after the war, in our "hey day" competition wasn't so fierce. There weren't so many small operators in the area and the big boys like Wallace Arnold, National Travel and Counties Travel served the main towns and left us to mop up in our own localities. Nowadays every village seems to have its own operator and the major operators have become more competitive every year.

'We've lived – and worked – through the birth and boom of extended British holidays and tours. We still do good business in this market but increasingly the public are looking to holiday abroad. They expect *luxury* travel, too, and you know that we've been hard pressed in recent years to maintain a reasonably modern fleet. At the same time customers are shopping around for price as well as quality and John will confirm that his quotations are often rejected by customers who've had better offers elsewhere.

'This year's balance sheet reflects the worsening profit situation and (for me this is the greatest worry) we all know that the Government's de-licensing legislation takes effect next year. The protection we've enjoyed on our licensed excursion and tours routes goes by the board next year. We will be involved in a free for all and the local competition has been wetting its lips in preparation for an all out attack on our established routes next year.

'In short, I'm suggesting that we've a serious situation on our hands. We've got to use a different approach to running this business. It's no use burying our heads and relying on hard work to make a living. None of us is getting any younger and I'm afraid that hard work alone is no longer a guarantee of success.

'One last thing; the four of us each earned £5,800 last year. In 1983, for the work and responsibility we incur that really is "peanuts" – and there hasn't been a dividend declared in years. I'm nearly 60 and you three aren't too far behind me. It's time we had a bit more to show for all the work and worry we've put in over the years.

'I've brought some financial information relating to our operations and – don't ask me how – I've managed to get hold of this year's accounts for Roadster Ltd (see Appendix 5.1). I think some of the figures in their accounts will surprise us and – importantly – help us to start thinking about where we are and where we want to be. I'd like to think we could start by improving the age of our fleet but you know we have consistently strained our overdraft limit of £15,000 over the past five years. The only way we've managed to balance our cash flow position has been through buying cheaper and older replacement coaches than we would otherwise have preferred.'

Scene 2 (around the same time as Scene 1)

Roadster Ltd is a small family-owned coach business presently operated by Hector Shaw (the son of the firm's founder) and Hector's son, Mark. The following text is extracts of a conversation which took place during a coffee break in the small booking office located at Roadster's premises.

HECTOR: 'Early bookings suggest that our licensed tours will do OK again this year and the new private hire contracts we secured during the 'off' season should help.'

MARK: 'Yes. If the weather is kind to us this year and helps us do well with the day and weekend work we should at least maintain last year's level of profit performance. But what about the longer term, Dad? You're 64 next month. Maybe it's time you were taking things easier. The signs are that times are going to get tougher in this industry.'

HECTOR: 'There's plenty of life left yet. Don't worry about me. I reckon that we're up to the new challenges. This firm grew up in a deregulated environment. We still get 60 per cent of our business in the freely competitive private hire sector and we have a good name. I think we can more than hold our own against the smaller independent opposition. They'll learn during the next couple of years that filling holiday coaches and day trips depends upon more than simply advertising a destination in the local papers.'

MARK: 'Yes, but we can't 'magic' a bigger community. There are only so many people to go round – and the big boys are becoming more professional and aggressive. This year we really have to look after our customers and to keep developing new private hire links. ...'

HECTOR: 'We would do a lot better, too, if we could get some co-operation from Counties Travel and Silver Wheels. It breaks my heart to see coaches from each organisation setting off to the same destination on the same day, each only one-third full.'

MARK: 'Yes, but you know I tried to get some collusion over who goes where and when. I'm sure with that sort of arrangement we could maintain turnover and reduce running costs by 10% or more. As it is, with all the independents trying to get a piece of the action things aren't likely to get any better. The drivers should be more settled, though, since we introduced the same wage rates as Counties Travel back at the beginning of 1983.'

HECTOR: 'We have a number of things going for us. I think it was an astute move on my part, giving you full rein when I reached 60. Since then I've watched the bank balance move slowly and surely from zero to around £20,000. Profits have improved and, in terms of British holidays and excursions, our fleet is the best around here.'

Scene 3 (around the same time as Scenes 1 and 2)

(The managing director's office – Counties Travel Ltd)

The managing director: 'Next year we lose the virtual monopoly we've held in this area so far as our licensed tours and excursion routes are concerned. Further, since we brought the Ravensthorpe to Anston services from Silver Wheels some years ago we have been the only operator undertaking stage carriage services but I confidently expect that the licensed protection we enjoy in this type of work will be removed by the present Government within the next three years. These licensed operations presently account for 20 per cent and 40 per cent of our total turnover, respectively. The remainder, as you know is roughly comprised of 30 per cent private hire and 10 per cent works contracts. If Government 'rate-capping' pressure gets any stronger I also suspect that we will be saying goodbye to the subsidies we receive from the County Council in return for our complying with their cheap fares policy. For the past ten years we have had things relatively easy. We've allowed a lot of "slack" to creep into our systems and we've not been mindful enough of the need to make useful profits. We have to change. On the one hand we will face increased local competition in our tours, excursions and stage carriage markets. On the other hand we can expect the more widely drawn companies of about our own size (120 buses/coaches) to re-route their British and Continental coach holidays to pick up in Anston. Of course, we in turn, can take the opportunity to market our own services in their areas. Whichever way we look at today's situation, however, we can see the need to change our presently over-bureaucratic and introverted methods of organising and operating.

'We also have to be alert to new opportunities. In this context I have two potential investment opportunities in mind at the moment. I'd appreciate your taking a look at them. ...

'You all know Silver Wheels and Roadster – two of our longer standing competitors. I think they might be ripe for takeover. They are the only operators around here (us apart) to hold any licences for excursions and tours. While they have never been big enough to really bother us they do, undoubtedly, take some of our business. Like us, they maintain a strong presence locally through being seen, through their use of local shops as booking agents, and through their network of well-established passenger picking up points. We have always maintained contact with both sets of directors – I had occasion to discuss some matters with them, separately, only last week.

'George Allen, particularly, is concerned about Silver Wheels' position these days. All the directors are in their mid- to late-50s, I guess, and while they are good 'old school' travel industry types I don't think they are up to handling effectively today's environments. In their early days I suppose they had thought that they were building up a viable business for their children but (quite sensibly, perhaps) it seems that the kids have moved on to greener occupational pastures. I think they might be ready to sell – if we are willing to buy. There might be some minor integration problems. Their coaches aren't up to our standards and I think their staff are on wage scales about 10 per cent below ours. There might also, of course, be some advantages. ...

'Roadster is, in many ways, a similar set up to Silver Wheels. This time, however, we'd be dealing with old Hector Shaw and his son, Mark. They are altogether sharper – Mark particularly is really on the ball. Hector is in his 60s though and the right sort of deal might tempt them to sell.

'I have copies of Roadster's and Silver Wheels' accounts (see Appendix 5.1) and I also have some industry average performance ratios (see Appendix 5.2). I'd like us to give some early thought to the financial and organisational issues involved in these potential acquisition strategies.'

Appendix 5.1 *Trading and profit and loss accounts*

| | Silver Wheels Ltd Years ended 31.12. 1982–83 | | Roadster Travel Ltd 31.12.83 |
	1982	1983	1983
Earnings	146,556	159,475	120,343
Deduct cost of earnings:			
Wages and National Insurance	44,082	47,829	28,963
Petrol, diesel, oil	30,749	33,017	18,206
Tyres	3,906	4,319	2,126
Spares	17,157	18,967	7,851
Parking fees/drivers' subsistence	3,648	3,480	3,241
Coaches hired in	9,051	9,106	2,634
Licences	1,314	2,090	1,200
Insurances	4,472	4,440	3,140
Stock – opening	5,483	7,411	2,001
	119,862	130,659	69,362
Less closing stock	7,411	8,076	2,224
	112,451	122,583	67,138

| | Silver Wheels Ltd Years ended 31.12. 1982–83 | | Roadster Travel Ltd 31.12.83 |
	1982	1983	1983
Gross profit	34,105	36,892	53,205
Add other income:			
Bank interest	8	28	–
Profit on sales of vehicles	9,327	7,484	15,000
	43,440	44,404	68,205
Deduct:			
Admin expenses			
Directors' remuneration	9,323	11,604	21,000
Postage and telephone	1,360	1,783	1,236
Painting and advertising	1,633	2,576	2,240
Audit charges	735	1,000	550
Subscriptions	98	155	–
Legal and professional charges	–	195	–
General expenses	–	–	1,000
Establishment charges			
Rates	1,291	1,569	1,400
Light and heat	1,876	2,765	2,165
Repairs and renewals	285	1,641	1,600
Financial expenses			
Bank charges	1,500	1,085	474
Discounts allowed to customers	1,539	1,641	431
HP interest	–	–	500
Depreciation			
Motor vehicles	12,818	13,606	16,100
Petrol pumps	3	3	–
Machinery	1	1	
	32,465	39,624	48,696
Net profit	10,978	4,780	19,509

Additional financial information

1 Silver Wheels wages include £11,604 (1983) for two of the four directors (these two are employed primarily as coach drivers rather than administrators).

2 Coaches are 'hired in' from other operators to cover excess demand in busy periods.

3 Profits on sales of vehicles is due largely to over depreciation in previous years.

4 HP interest (see Roadster account) has accrued, following the purchase from another operator, of a coach which was subject to an HP agreement.

5 Previous Silver Wheels net profits have been £14,036 (1978); £20,501 (1979); £16,402 (1980); £18,791 (1981).

	Silver-Wheels Ltd balance sheet 31.12.83		Roadster Ltd balance sheet 31.12.83	
Fixed assets				
Land and building				
(at cost 1953)	8217		15,000 (1958)	
Petrol pumps	26		–	
Plant	2		–	
Loose tools	1,156		–	
Fixtures and fittings	592		1,212	
Motor vehicles	55,896		80,000	
		65,889		96,212
Current assets				
Stock	8,076		1,224	
Debts and prepayments	25,541		10,211	
Cash and bank balance	2,764		19,326	
	36,381		30,761	
Current liabilities				
Creditors	23,501		15,932	
Bank overdraft	14,643		–	
Finance company loan	–		5,000	
Directors current accounts	13,770		35,000	
	51,914	(15,533)	55,932	(25,171)
		50,356		71,041
Share capital		1,000		10,000
Retained earnings		45,759		61,041
Capital Reserve		3,597		–
		50,356		71,041

Additional balance sheet information

1   Land and buildings (for both organisations) now stand at £60,000 (current valuations) although Silver Wheels has three times the area of land (much of it unused) and bigger garage and office blocks.
2   Silver Wheels has 10 Bedford/Plaxton coaches; the newest 5 years old, the oldest 10 years old.
3   Roadster has 6 Bedford/Plaxton coaches; the newest 2 years old, the oldest 5 years old.
4   Directors' current accounts are composed of loans made to the companies, over the years, by the directors.
5   Stock consists of petrol, diesel, oil, tyres and spares.

Other generally known information

1   Silver Wheels has a particularly good (price-wise) contract for petrol, diesel and oil.
2   Roadster's two directors are concerned mainly with planning and administration.

3   Silver Wheels earns revenue from the following sources:

* Works contracts (NCB, local factories, etc.) and school services (2 coaches are employed 5 days per week on these services)
* Day, weekend and extended British excursions, tours and holidays. Licensed (rather than private hire) operations in these areas accounted for approximately 30 per cent of turnover. However, profit contribution breakdowns have never been attempted.

4   Roadster has almost identical markets except that it does not operate any works or school contracts.

Appendix 5.2 *Some industry performance standards*

Current ratio	1.1
Gearing	50%
Interest cover ratio	11.0
Fixed charge cover ratio	5.0
Stock control	25
Permanent asset turnover ratio	2.0
ROCE	10%
ROS	12%
ROE	44%
Gross profit margin	35%
Fuel to earnings	17%
Average seating capacity full (licensed excursions, tours and holidays)	80%
Admin expenses to sales	20%

Appendix 5.3 *Counties Travel, Silver Wheels and Roadster geographical relationship*

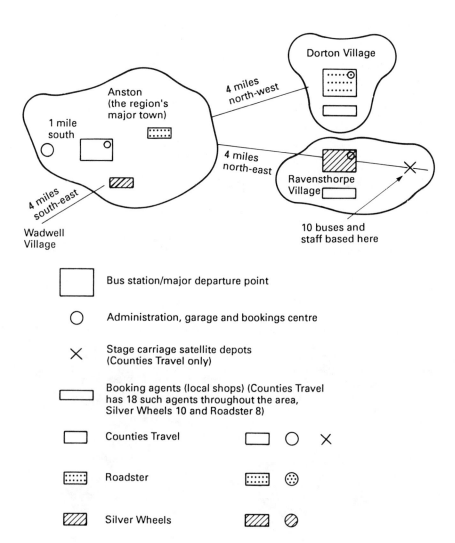

Appendix 5.4 *Counties Travel – 1984 expenditure budget for satellite bus depot at Ravensthorpe*

	£
	£
Wages and salaries	66,000
Petrol, diesel and oil	40,000
Spares and repairs	20,000
Licences and insurance	7,000
Miscellaneous	2,500
Telephone	1,000
Rates	2,000
Light and heat	4,000
	£142,500

Value of land and premises £40,000 (recent internal evaluation)

Salaries/wages:	
Depot Manager	10,000
Foreman/Assistant Manager	7,500
Drivers (per driver)	5,800

Appendix 5.5 *Counties Travel Ltd: executive structure*

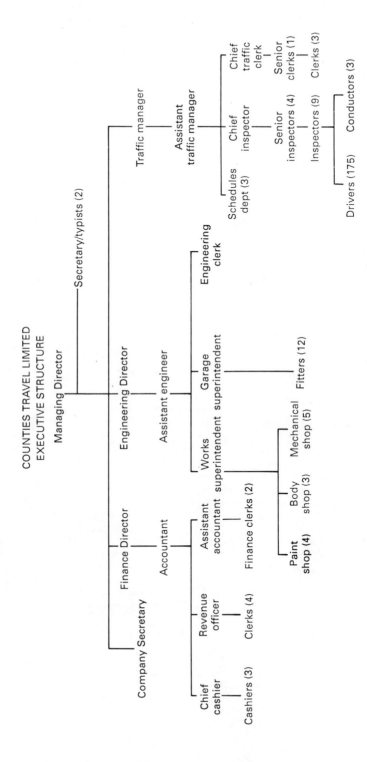

COUNTIES TRAVEL LIMITED
EXECUTIVE STRUCTURE

Managing Director

Secretary/typists (2)

Finance Director

Engineering Director

Traffic manager

Company Secretary

Accountant

Assistant engineer

Assistant traffic manager

Chief cashier

Revenue officer

Assistant accountant

Works superintendent

Garage superintendent

Engineering clerk

Schedules dept (3)

Chief inspector

Chief traffic clerk

Cashiers (3)

Clerks (4)

Finance clerks (2)

Paint shop (4)

Body shop (3)

Mechanical shop (5)

Fitters (12)

Senior inspectors (4)

Senior clerks (1)

Drivers (175)

Inspectors (9)

Clerks (3)

Conductors (3)

Section 3 · Consumer and leisure products

6 · Everlasting Hardware plc

Maurice Brown and John Patterson

Everlasting Hardware plc is a recently acquired subsidiary of an American multinational holding company. The company is functionally structured and located on a single site in south-west England, with a resident managing director. Most of the senior and middle management (including the managing director) has long service records with Everlasting, going back before the takeover. One important exception to this is the marketing manager, an American who was brought into the firm at the insistence of the holding company, just over a year ago. Since the takeover Everlasting has operated independently of the group, providing most services in-house.

The main links between subsidiary and group are via a Group Audit Committee which annually reviews individual subsidiary performance and the Group Capital Budget Committee which vets all project proposals in excess of £250,000 and annual capital budget requests from subsidiaries in excess of £2m. Companies within the group are required to repatriate 60 per cent of annual profit to the holding company and have discretionary disposal over the remaining 40 per cent within the parameters indicated. Allocation of funds from the holding company are treated as commercial debt and subsidiaries are actively discouraged from gearing up beyond 50 per cent. Experience to date has indicated that although group policy is to focus strongly on ROCE performance of subsidiaries the audit committee positively encourages product and market diversification/growth, and inter-subsidiary competition for funds.

Everlasting manufactures a long-established and well-known range of kitchen utensils which has a good reputation for quality and reliability. The range has not, however, been substantially changed over the past ten years, and has increasingly been regarded as 'old fashioned' by younger purchasers, who have tended to turn to imported products from France and Sweden. The firm has an established policy that not more than 50 per cent, by value, of components will be bought in.

In an effort to improve its image, the firm is investing in the manufacture of a new high quality range of saucepans, which will sell alongside its existing range, but at a higher price. For its existing range the manufacture of handles is contracted to an external supplier. However, for this new range the MD feels that it would be a good opportunity to acquire in-house expertise. It is envisaged that the specifications of the new handles will improve on existing standards of heat resistance, texture, design and colours. The newly developed polymers used in injection moulding the plastics have recently been patented and these patents could be purchased to prevent a competitor from developing a similar handle. The main problem for Everlasting is its lack of expertise in injection moulding; eg in processing high grade plastics, temperature control is vital if degradation is to be avoided. The operation of the injection moulding equipment is a highly skilled task and it takes six to nine months of training to produce operatives of an adequate standard. Twelve operatives will be needed to run the plant on two shifts. The nearest supply of trained labour is in the north-east of England, where similar plant is operated, but good workers are in short supply and command premium rates. It will also be necessary to recruit two technicians to supervise the day-to-day running of the plant, and here again good people are in very short supply. Such technicians normally have a degree in chemical engineering and are typically appointed at middle management level, reporting directly to the production manager.

The views of departmental heads have been thoroughly explored in the Product Development and Approval Committee. The managing director, who is under pressure from the holding company to improve the image of Everlasting's products, is in favour of in-house manufacture, since he sees future uses of the process for other products. The marketing manager shares his view, seeing the new material as crucial for the firm's long-term product/market strategy. There is, however, strong opposition from the production manager and his staff, who favour buying in the new handles to avoid unnecessary disruption. The personnel manager also has severe reservations about the training and recruitment programme needed for in-house manufacture. Despite these conflicting views, appropriate financial and technical estimates have been produced, and these yield the following conclusions:

1 The product is thought to have a life-cycle of no more than ten years.
2 The polymer patents can be purchased for £120,000 (or licences obtained for £5,000 per year).
3 Unused space within the factory is available for the installation of new machinery. (This space has no alternative use.)
4 Tooling up and ancillary expenditure, ie the purchase and installation of an injection moulding machine, is estimated at £500,000.
5 Everlasting's traditional supplier could be used instead of in-house manufacture in which case the purchasing officer is confident that he can negotiate a long-term contract price of about £20 per set of handles.
6 If the range remains in production for nine years or more initial costs will be entirely written off and machinery will have a zero scrap value, if eight years £2,500 and if six years, a scrap value of about £10,000.
7 Manufacturing costs per set of handles have been estimated as follows:

Years $t1$ to $t3$ inclusive: throughout this period there may be production run and quality control problems caused by lack of experience:

Unit costs build-up:

	Normal production	Severe problems	No problems
Materials	£1.00	£1.75	£0.75
Direct labour	6.00	7.00	4.35
Fuel and power	0.50	0.75	0.40
Overhead*	2.50	2.50	2.50
Allocated general exps	0.90	0.90	0.90
Depreciation	7.00	7.00	7.00
	£17.90	£19.90	£15.90

Years t4 to t10 inclusive: during this period there should be no problems and it can 'safely' be assumed that unit costs will be no more than £16 per set of handles.

The above calculations are based on an annual target of 11,000 sets of good handles per year (unit variable costs are constant in the range of 6,000–12,000 sets per year).

8   At the end of the product's life all staff hired should be retained within the company. There is, however, a small chance that some will be made redundant and that severance costs should be allowed for. If the project folds in t9 or t10 these would be £20,000, in t8 £15,000, or if it folds as early as t6 they could be much higher due to the difficulty of redeploying the numbers involved, say £60,000.

9   Under the current tax regime all initial outlays on patent purchase and tooling up can be written off on a 25 per cent reducing balance basis over eight years. The corporation tax rate is 35 per cent.

10   Sales of the final product are quite sensitive to the business cycle, in recession they could average as low as 4,000 sets per year, whereas in boom times they could be as high as 14,000 sets per year, and in normal conditions annual sales should be around 11,000 sets.

Other issues discussed by the appraisal committee revolved around problems likely to be faced if the patent is not purchased – the difficulty of working to tighter specification on a new component in which the company has no experience and the difficulties of quality control in the early stages of operation. The marketing manager considered the purchase of the patent to be crucial because he knew of several rival companies which were also considering up-grading their brands. If this happened it could be assumed that Everlasting's sales would be around 75 per cent of the predicted levels. The

* Overhead is broken down into the provision of training for direct labour from t1 to t3 and hiring of additional supervisors for the life of the product:

Training allocation	£0.50
Supervision	2.00
	£2.50

senior production manager was quite confident that learning problems would be minimal and that production would be 'normal' after about six months, his line-foremen were not so sanguine and were arguing for considerably more conservative cost estimates. The purchasing manager responsible for capital items estimated a full year from order-installation and commissioning before the production of handles would be on stream. Hanging over the committee was the knowledge that the managing director was expecting a positive report to take to the Group Capital Budget Committee.

To incorporate the numerous uncertainties the appraisal committee decided that some kind of sensitivity analysis was essential and a newly appointed young graduate in the marketing team suggested the expectational approach he had been schooled in at his polytechnic. He explained to the appraisal team that essentially this meant 'weighting' the possible outcomes by the 'likelihood' of their occurrence and estimating the weighted average value/outcome or as he called it the 'expected value'. He demonstrated that 'weightings' were based on management perceptions of the environment and persuaded the committee to co-operate. The results are listed below:

Production t1 to t3

	Probability*	Unit costs
Severe problems	0.5	£19.90
Normal production	0.4	17.90
No problems	0.1	15.90

* Disputed by the production managers' (apart from the senior manager) more pessimistic view

State of the economy

	Probability	Annual sales
Recession	0.25	4,000
Normal	0.5	9,000
Boom	0.25	12,000

Redundancy

	Probability
Redundancy	0.3
No redundancy	0.7

Project life

	Probability
10 years	0.6
8 years	0.3
6 years	0.1

More pragmatic managers also insisted on a more traditional and 'easy to understand' approach simply identifying key factors and measuring viability against different assumed values of these.

Appendix 6.1 *Group-subsidiary control chart*

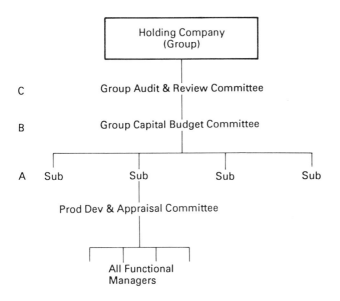

A   60 per cent of all profit repatriated to group, discretionary use over rest subject to parameters in B.

B   All projects >£250,000 must be submitted from subsidiaries for vetting. Annual capital budgets >£2m must be approved. The company imposed cost of capital on fund allocations is 20 per cent.

C   Reviews subsidiary performance. Main measure ROCE, but also emphasise on market and product growth/diversification.

Appendix 6.2 *Industiral relations at Everlasting*

The firm employs a total of 250 people on a single site. There has been a long history of bad industrial relations at Everlasting, and the company has experienced several major disputes. Prior to the takeover by an American holding company three years ago, Everlasting had always refused formally to recognise any trade union, and was notorious for low wages and bad working conditions. As a result of this, labour turnover was, and indeed remains very high. Morale at shop-floor level had never been good, with most workers taking an anti-company stance and complaining of 'high-handed' and autocratic managements. After the takeover, Head Office in the USA insisted on union recognition, in line with its corporate policy, and the firm now pays minimum union rates throughout the plant.

There have been two strikes since the takeover. The first of these was a dispute about the 'clocking-in' system following a move by management to deduct one hour's pay if any employee was late twice in the same week.

Production was stopped for three weeks before the matter was resolved. The second strike was less protracted and began when an engineer and two labourers were given instant dismissal because of alleged abuse of a foreman. The men were reinstated on orders from the managing director after four days.

The managing director is generally regarded as very reactionary, but has had to modify his approach in recent years to avoid undue intervention from Head Office. He viewed the appointment of the new marketing manager (who has replaced most of the marketing staff) as a warning of further changes to come if he did not resolve some of the firm's long-term problems. Other managers wish to continue with their 'traditional' methods of working and urge him to take a harder line with Head Office, which they believe would 'back-off' in the event of a showdown. Whilst the managing director is sympathetic to their attitudes he also believes that change will have to come and does not want to lose his job in the process.

These disputes at senior management level have had unfortunate effects on middle management which is generally dispirited and lacks a sense of direction. Marketing staff aside, most of them feel that union recognition and the generally 'softer' line have made matters worse, in that the discipline they are used to imposing is now openly resented and resisted by the workforce.

7 · Beecham Group plc and SmithKline Beecham plc

John Patterson and June Cattermole

An excellent example of a multinational UK manufacturing company that was forced into a major strategic reappraisal between 1986 and 1989 is Beecham plc. The review culminated in a merger with the American pharmaceutical company SmithKline-Beckman in July 1989 and is not yet complete. Whilst the reappraisal was undoubtedly painful in its immediate consequences - business divestments, organisational restructuring and management replacement - it was essential to pre-empt a break-up hostile takeover bid. The changes were rooted in a poorly implemented growth strategy since the 1960s which resulted in a weakening financial performance and a progressive loss of top management control over strategic decisions.

Beecham has traditionally been regarded as a sound, well-managed, if somewhat conservative, company – the type which for decades was the backbone of British industry. Historically its business growth and market performance was viewed as satisfactory, but lacking the sparkle of star performers of the 1980s such as Owen Green's BTR. However, since 1982 market analysts have viewed its performance as less than modest. From the following extracts from company records it can be seen that the 'bottom line' indicates a sharp deterioration, and if inflation is taken into account the flat EPS performance is illusory. It was not until the strategic review was well into its implementation phase that the overall company performance began to improve.

To appreciate why the company came to the point in 1985 when its top management felt impelled to initiate a full-scale strategic review of the business portfolio, it is beneficial to trace central features of the historic growth of the group.

A public company for over sixty years, Beecham had grown from a modest base as a producer of laxatives and over-the-counter medicines (OTC) before the Second World War, into a multinational conglomerate manufacturing and distributing a wide range of ethical drugs, proprietary medicines and general consumer products. From 1945 growth was consistent – in pharmaceuticals largely organic, and in general consumer products mainly by acquisition. Acquisitions increased in the 1970s as Beecham bought into production and distribution on a global scale in order to by-pass the increasing complexities of greenfield start-ups in highly regulated overseas ethical drug industries, for example, the USA and West Germany.

Year	Turnover	£millions Trading profit	Net assets employed	Before tax return on sales	Before tax return on net assets	£s Earnings per share	1980 = 100 Inflation Adjusted EPs
1981	1194.7	161.0	738.8	13.48%	21.79%	0.14	0.119
1982	1407.0	204.6	832.5	14.54%	24.58%	0.18	0.144
1983	1702.4	243.5	1059.5	14.30%	22.98%	0.22	0.168
1984	1944.0	270.9	1284.1	13.94%	21.10%	0.22	0.158
1985	2289.1	321.5	1577.5	14.04%	20.38%	0.23	0.157
1986	2627.1	340.0	1776.4	12.94%	19.14%	0.24	0.152
1987	2769.5	399.8	1791.4	14.44%	22.32%	0.27	0.169
1988	2480.2	464.5	1903.9	18.73%	24.40%	0.32	0.190

In organisational terms the group was structured into Beecham Pharmaceuticals and Beecham Consumer Products operating under separate managing directors reporting to a common executive chairman. The separation of control from top board level management was such that:

- the businesses were quasi-independent and used to presenting strategic plans to the executive committee for rubber stamping rather than negotiation;
- there were no formal communication links to ensure that the two businesses marched in tandem.

Some city analysts likened the businesses to 'feudal baronies' and put this loss of central control and lack of communication at the heart of the traumas of 1986. An examination of the skeleton of the business structure gives an insight into the problems of dovetailing a vast array of products.

Beecham Pharmaceuticals

* Ethical drugs (cash cows): penicillin based antibiotics, eg Amoxil and Penbriton (patents expire late 1980s)

* Ethical drugs (cash stars): broad spectrum drugs to address penicillin resistant bacteria, eg Augmentin, Synulox and Timentin (launched 1985)

* Ethical drugs (question marks): anti arthritis, Nabumetone; cardiovascular, Eminase

* Proprietary medicines (cash cows): Beecham's Pills, Beecham's Powders, Venos Cough Mixture, Germolene, Vitamins (and other brandnames)

Beecham Consumer Products

* Personal care products (several tired brand names): Brylcreem, Silvikrin, Macleans toothpaste, and Aqua Fresh toothpaste (all acquired before 1950); Calgon, acquired in 1977

* Cosmetic products: Jovan, Yardley, Lentheric, Mornay, Monteil (all acquired between 1979 and 1985)

* Home improvement products: Copydex, Unibond, Uhu and DAP

* Food and drink products: Lucozade, Ribena, Bovril (1980) Horlicks (1969), Corona, Tango, Quosh, Idris, Hunts; Franchises and agencies eg Coca Cola bottling, Campari, Remy Martin; Findlater and Mackie Todd retail outlets; Batchelors foods (Ireland)

The list is not exhaustive, but it does give a flavour of the spread of products and brand names and gives credence to the view of a progressive loss of focus and the move to conglomerate status.

The development of the consumer products side of the group lacked strategic coherence. For example, the purchase of Horlicks in 1969 included a dairy distribution business in south-west England. Horlicks fitted neatly into the range of health drinks and sensibly should have divested the dairy side but did not. Similarly, the popular adhesive Uhu came along with the acquisition of Fischer & Fischer, a German toiletry company. The personal care fit of toiletries is obvious but in holding on to Uhu Beecham by default got into DIY. This was the essence of Beecham's acquisition trail from 1960 until well into the 1980s. Acquisitions were rarely followed by the divestment of unwanted bits of acquired companies and between 1960 and 1986 Beecham did not make a single significant divestment.

Thus, although the company appeared to pursue a coherent acquisition strategy, it was not accompanied by a coherent divestment strategy. As a consequence the business was saddled with several tired brands and an expensive launch into the DIY sector with predictable disappointing financial results, although within this, brands like Uhu and Copydex performed well.

It is pertinent to ask why after two decades of growth did performance falter in the early 1980s to the extent that exposure to a break-up predator became a distinct possibility. The group, after all, had a reputation for strong brand management and had developed an enviable reputation in the specialist marketing and distribution of ethical drugs which should have continued to compensate for an inadequate divestment strategy.

Paradoxically the cause was rooted in the pharmaceutical side of the company. Although ethical drugs, if successful, have very high sales margins, they also have extremely long gestation periods from research laboratory to the chemist's shelf. Beecham's penicillin range was launched in the late 1950s and was hugely successful on a worldwide scale. Whilst sales margins on consumer products were relatively modest in the intensely competitive toiletry, cosmetic, DIY, and drink markets (eg Macleans toothpaste was actually withdrawn from the US market), the successful penicillin range was still generating attractive margins in the 1970s. It was the latter which maintained the group's overall margin on sales above 13 per cent, the average on consumer products being around 10 per cent. Of course investment in drugs is high risk. The apparent balance in the portfolio became increasingly disturbed in the late 1970s and early 1980s:

- In 1970 pharmaceuticals accounted for 40 per cent of turnover and 60 per cent of trading profit. By 1984 this had reduced to 30 per cent of turnover and 50 per cent of profit.
- In 1985 about 80 per cent of the pharmaceutical income was derived from the Amoxil range which was within three years of patent expiry.
- Major investments were increasingly biased towards consumer products, eg the acquisition of BAT's cosmetic business for £125m as opposed to the £40m invested in the new drug plant at Irvine in Scotland.

- The hitherto attractive margins on the now dated range of ethical drugs came under pressure: approaching end of patent life; increased pirating; tighter procurement policies in the NHS.
- Longer delays in getting new drugs approved had doubled the costs from laboratory to chemist shelf since the 1960s.

Sir Ronald Halstead, the chief executive until his abrupt removal in November 1985, said 'the more rigorous NHS pricing policy had reduced the ROCE on pharmaceuticals to below the average for UK industry.' This coupled with the over reliance on its penicillin range of antibiotics and the mistiming in getting the replacement drugs on stream – the important antiarthritic and cardiovascular drugs would not be available until the late 1980s – meant that the emerging profit gap would have to be covered by consumer products. The failure of the DIY products and weakness of the cosmetic range, particularly in America, combined to produce the flat performance after 1982, and was the catalyst for the strategic rethink that was to follow. Remarks made by the senior non-executive director, Lord Keith, at the time of Halstead's forced resignation indicate the strength of the reaction: 'management did not look with any thoroughness at where the business expected to be in seven years time. For the first time we are saying "do we really want to be in that business?" '

Three strategic decisions were taken:

1   To concentrate the business portfolio on three areas in which Beecham had a distinctive competence:
    - pharmaceuticals
    - personal care products
    - general health products.
2   To divest peripheral businesses, vacate markets in which performance was weak, and use the proceeds to reduce gearing and plough into drug R&D.
3   To institute organisationsal changes which would:
    - generate comprehensive business and product audits;
    - give more authority to the executive committee to vet major acquisitions;
    - limit the tenure of non-executive directors;
    - increase the accountability of executive directors.

It was quickly decided that Beecham should concentrate on managing the type of branded products it knows best and give a much stronger focus to diversifying the development of new ethical drug products. The divestment programme was ruthless and almost complete in the space of one year:

- Rehein Chemicals (USA) sold as a management buyout for $23.5m
- Horlicks Farms and Dairies sold to Unigate for £5.8m
- Batchelors Foods (Ireland) sold to Northern Foods for £12.5m
- The Ace Comb Company and Australian Soft Drinks sold to Goody Products (Australia) for £12m

- Corona, Tango, Hunts, Idris brands sold to Britvic for £120m
- Coca-Cola bottling and distribution sold to Cadbury-Schweppes for $10m
- The home improvement and DIY business broken up and sold for a total of £200m

By the beginning of 1987 only the Monteil perfumery subsidiary and the Findlater and Mackie Todd drink distribution and retail outlets had not found buyers. Total disposals for 1986 raised £366m. The loss making businesses, Monteil (US), and Beecham Cosmetics (US) were sold in late 1987.

An important feature of the divestments is that without exception they went to companies in the same business sector or as stand alone management buyouts, a sharp contrast to the conglomerate philosophy of the previous two decades.

That a degree of market confidence was restored in the management of Beecham was evidenced by the increase in the P/E multiple from 13 at the time of Halstead's resignation to a range between 20 to 25 by the end of 1986, substantially eliminating any takeover benefit. The point to emphasise is that whilst Beecham was not in financial distress it had progressively lost portfolio focus and senior management direction with the consequent effect of under performing businesses acting as a drag on the group as a whole. This led to persistent rumours that ICI was interested in the pharmaceutical business and Unilever in some of the consumer products. To this extent the radical strategic review should be seen as not just overdue but as a defensive reaction against potential takeover threats.

In August 1986 an American, Bob Bauman, was appointed to replace Halstead as group chief executive, the overall managing director was to be John Robb the former consumer products division managing director. Bauman initiated a two-year divestment programme accompanied by the necessary organisational and managerial restructuring to ensure a dilution in the influence of senior management at divisional level which had been a characteristic of the 'old' Beecham for so many years. Restructuring meant that all the newly appointed divisional chiefs would in future report directly to Bauman. John Robb saw this as an unacceptable erosion of his own power base and resigned in September 1988.

The slimmed down Beecham was ultimately intended to have the following structure:

Pharmaceuticals
- Ethical drugs
- Proprietary (OTC) medicines, eg Venos, Germolene, Beecham's Pills, Beecham's Powders

Personal care
- eg Brylcreem, Silvikrin, Badedas, Yardley, Jovan

Health products
- eg Lucozade, Ribena, Horlicks, Bovril

For Bauman, R&D strategy was to be the central feature of the new Beecham. He considered that the company had lost sight of its core business, had become over dependent on the antibiotics introduced in the 1950s, and had fallen well behind market leaders such as Glaxo in product innovation. R&D expenditure was increased from £63m in 1985 to £95m in 1988. At the same time advertising and promotion was increased on long-established 'health' products such as Lucozade to restore market lustre.

By way of comparison Glaxo was, in 1989, moving up the FT 100 from 72 to 64 and Beecham at the same time was moving down from 39 to 52. The following extracts indicates the performance margin between the two companies:

1986 data £m	Beecham	Glaxo
Turnover	2480.2	2059.1
Trading profit	464.5	858.1
Return on sales	18.7%	41.7%
ROCE	24.4%	46.7%
Market capitalisation	4820.6	10164.2
Employees	35800	26423

The American dimension became stronger with the appointment of J Andress as managing director of pharmaceuticals, and in 1989 Bauman gave a further twist to the strategic reassessment by deciding to steer Beecham towards a merger with SmithKline Beckman to create the second largest player in the global drugs market. The rationale for the proposed merger was based on synergistic expectations; a complementary product portfolio, joint R&D, common distribution channels, and a stronger profile not only in the traditional European and American markets but also in the emerging high income markets of the Pacific Rim.

The new Anglo-American company SmithKline Beecham plc was formed in July 1989 under the joint leadership of Bob Bauman as chief executive and Henry Wendt (ex SmithKline) as chairman, both Americans. Although the new group would have equal numbers of top managers drawn from the two cons-ituent companies the major strategic control and flavour would be American for Wendt insisted that pharmaceuticals be fronted by an American. The other, now downgraded, business areas would be headed by Beecham executives. Head Office would be split between Brentford (UK) and Pittsburgh (USA).

The merger value was over £9bn and the consolidating costs of £500m in funding workforce redundancies of 10 per cent and substantial site rationalisation would be spread over three years. One immediate effect for Beecham was that its pre-merger gearing rose from 40 per cent to over 100 per cent of shareholders' funds.

The short-term effects of the merger resulted in a weakening financial performance as the joint return on sales fell sharply in 1989 to 16.7 per cent, well behind the industry norm. Analysts put the problem down to two causes.

First, the underestimation of the difficulty of marrying disparate corporate cultures and the managerial uncertainties created by the rationalisation programme – it was pointed out that the Ciba-Geigy merger took several years to settle down. Second, the combined drug portfolios were still unbalanced in terms of patent life and competitive products available from companies like Glaxo and Merck. Indeed SmithKline's hitherto best-selling ulcer drug, Tagamet, fell prey to ferocious competition from Glaxo and Eli Lilley and it was suggested that in reality Beecham was a White Knight.

In early 1990 the interest burden of the high gearing forced the company into further disposals in order to reduce gearing. For example, historically famous brands in the original Beecham's portfolio, such as Marmite, Bovril and Ambrosia were put up for sale (ostensibly because they did not fit into the new healthcare portfolio), as well as off-patent drugs and the rump of the cosmetics businesses. Altogether little more than £500m was raised.

8 · Steinman Print

Anthea Gregory

Background

Steinman Print was founded by Joshua Steinman and his wife, Ruby, in 1980. Joshua had many years experience in the printing industry and had previously owned another company which had gone into liquidation in the mid-1970s as a result of the economic recession.

In order to start up Steinman Print, Joshua's family provided the necessary capital. The new venture started off quite successfully and in 1984 Joshua and Ruby employed John Wyatt to help Joshua manage the factory. Ruby, meanwhile, looked after the accounts and administration of the company with the help of her retired father on a part-time basis. John was considered 'one of the best in the business' and soon the performance of the company showed significant improvement. In order to retain John, Joshua made him a director of Steinman Print and he took a 10 per cent share in the company.

In 1989 Steinman Print expanded into a new factory equipped with new machinery paid for by the surplus funds which the company had generated.

The printing company

The company specialised in the printing of law textbooks and open learning material. These are relatively low price products but are high volume. Steinman Print had built a good reputation in this market and had 5 or 6 large customers who took the majority of the company's output.

By the end of 1990 the company had established itself in its new environment and continued to make healthy profits. It was at this point that Joshua decided they should start to look to the future. Although the company was doing well and had loyal customers Joshua knew from previous experience that its narrow product and market focus made the company vulnerable.

Joshua, Ruby and John decided to identify areas of weakness in the organisation and outline how these could be tackled. Three main problems came to light in their analysis of the situation. First, there was spare capacity in the new factory; second, their product and customer base was too narrow; and third, the factory would only efficiently produce its current narrow product range.

They identified the following courses of action. First, they decided to employ a sales representative who was to find new customers with printing requirements similar to their current customers. This would use the factory's spare capacity and increase their customer base. They therefore advertised the post which was eventually filled. Second, they decided that in order to spread their risk they should diversify although at this stage they had no clear idea of what form this diversification might take.

The shop

During this period Joshua saw a photocopy/printing shop advertised for sale. This shop was situated between two main tube and railway stations and was surrounded by office blocks. The area was undergoing major redevelopment with new office blocks under construction across the road. The products and services offered by the shop included self-service copying, colour copying, plan copying, bulk copying, artwork and typesetting, printing and office stationery. The shop's accounts showed it to be making large profits and it was feasible that Steinman Print could meet the asking price, even though it would stretch its borrowing facility to the limit.

Joshua thought this was an ideal diversification as the shop operations were related to the mainstream business of the organisation, ie printing, but operating in another market, ie retailing. He was soon able to persuade Ruby and John that this opportunity was too good to pass over and the purchase of the shop went ahead.

The lease of the shop and its equipment was signed over to Steinman Print at the beginning of June 1990. The purchase price was approx £250,000. For this Steinman Print took over the leasehold of the shop, the leasing agreements on the copying equipment, one small printing press, the stock of stationery and customer goodwill. Steinman Print also retained all the staff at the shop.

One year later the shop had failed to make any profit. It was significantly below budget on turnover and coupled with this were the problems of very high overheads which they had to sustain. After twelve months of making losses they decided they needed help to turn the shop around as it was creating a cash drain on the organisation and despite a number of initiatives they had been unable to stop this situation persisting.

The DTI were prepared to subsidise the cost of bringing consultants into the organisation and so two consultants were engaged to conduct a preliminary analysis of the situation. It was decided that it would be necessary to conduct a strategic and financial analysis of the organisation. Having been given the above background to the problem the consultants outlined a number of areas for investigation. Listed below is the information the consultants collected (although not their analysis).

Discussions with the directors

(abridged transcripts from interviews with the directors)

Joshua Steinman, interview

QUESTION: What do you feel the major problems are for the shop?

ANSWER: There are two main problems. First, the shop is carrying very large overheads in terms of the leasehold of the shop and the leasing agreements on the copying equipment. Added to this most of the copying equipment is idle for a large proportion of the time, particularly the bulk copiers. We have two of these but really we only have enough work to utilise one. We tried to get out of the leasing agreement but the leasing company wasn't interested in taking the equipment back. The agreement still has a number of years to run so we are unable to reduce our overheads.

Also we are employing a lot of people to run the shop. We have a manager, James. He is 24 which is quite young but he has had prior experience of running shops like this and is familiar with most of the equipment and so fills in for other staff when they are off. There is Bryan who does the bulk copying, a senior and junior typesetter, David, who does the printing and Jill who operates the till and also orders the stationery stock. We are making Jill redundant though as we have decided that Ruby should work down at the shop 2–3 days a week. It is unfortunate that Ruby isn't capable of managing the shop, but she hasn't the time really as we need her at the factory to do the wages and credit control.

The second problem is that we are not achieving the level of sales we expected. The previous owner had sales turnover in excess of £30,000 per month but we haven't achieved anything like this. Part of the problem is that the previous owner took most of his customers with him and now services them from the other copy bureaux which he owns. Of course he took his customer lists with him so we don't even know who those customers are. On top of this the current recession means that people are more cost conscious. Now they do most of their copying on their own copiers and they keep their printed work to a minimum and indeed many have their own desk top publishing systems.

QUESTION: What do you feel the future prospects are for the shop?

ANSWER: I know the shop could make a profit. It did before so there is no reason why it can't now. The printing press we have down there seems to be fully utilised so it may be an idea to expand that side of the shop's business. If we did this maybe we would need to get a sales rep. to drum up custom.

John Wyatt interview

QUESTION: What do you feel the major problems are for the shop?

ANSWER: Simple – it's not making any money and is acting as a cash drain on our main operations. If Joshua or I had time we could probably go down there and sort it out. But as things are at the factory this is not possible. I am not sure that even this would work. I think that maybe we just made a bad decision. When we bought the shop Joshua was so keen he carried the rest of us along with the idea. I wish we hadn't gone ahead with the purchase but it would be very difficult to sell at the moment, despite the redevelopment in the area, and we would not realise anything like the amount we paid for it.

QUESTION: What do you feel the future prospects are for the shop?

ANSWER: We will have to divert more of the small run printing work from the factory to the shop. We have already done this with work for one of our customers and I am sure that they are now one of the shop's largest customers. We have to stay with the current line of work in the shop due to the leasing agreements. We have to pay for the leases whether the equipment is used or not.

Ruby Steinman interview

QUESTION: What do you feel the major problems are for the shop?

ANSWER: I don't really know. I have been working in the shop for some weeks now and there doesn't seem to be any pattern to the business. Some days we are rushed off our feet with all the copiers working flat out and other days we don't even turn them on. On the other hand the stationery is pretty constant so perhaps our focus is wrong. I feel we should try and sell cards and fancy goods. There are plenty of people from the local offices who pass by. We have started selling cards and at Christmas they did really well so I think we should extend our range. I also stocked notelets, briefcases, picture frames and 'fancy' stationery but these don't seem to have sold so well – the customers don't seem interested, but we have some really lovely stuff.

QUESTION: What do you feel the future prospects are for the shop?

ANSWER: I think if we can increase our range of stationery then our sales will increase.

Competition

Steinman Print seem unaware of their competition. The consultants carried out a brief survey of competitors in the vicinity of the shop.

There are approximately ten copy/print shops within a quarter of a mile radius of the shop offering similar or the same goods/services. All of them said that their main customers were local businesses that primarily used their services for convenience and speed, rather than trying to carry out bulk copying on their own photocopiers, or for quality, which again could not be achieved on their own copiers.

All of the competition expressed concern about the current recession and its affect on their business. However, the ones that were faring best said that they were now pricing more competitively by offering discounts and were actively promoting their businesses either with mail shots, fliers or, in one particular case, through employing a sales representative.

Competitors' prices were not dissimilar to Steinman Print's. The premises of franchised shops, eg Pronta Print were generally clean, bright and pleasant.

Customer perceptions

A survey was conducted by the consultants. Their findings can be summarised as follows.

Customers were generally unaware of the full range of goods and services on offer in the shop. Most customers considered the shop 'unattractive' and it was difficult to find what they wanted. Opinions about prices differed depending on the type of customer. Business customers thought the shop was expensive especially for stationery items. Customers making personal purchases thought the prices were competitive. All customers thought that the shop's staff offered a good service.

The business customers interviewed normally went elsewhere for the goods they purchased at the shop but had used the shop on this particular occasion as it was close and they needed the goods/services quickly.

Promotion

Steinman Print has tried a couple of mail shots but these have proved ineffective. However, these were not targeted at specific business types nor at particular geographical areas. (The mail shots themselves were not particularly well designed and gave details of the shop's equipment rather than an outline of the benefits of using their services, eg speed, convenience, quality.)

Product mix

The shop is capable of providing a comprehensive range of copying and printing services and has a wide range of office stationery. Unfortunately there is a lack of focus in Steinman Print's purchasing policy and a large number of lines have been tried which are not consistent with the shop's main business, ie. a provider of goods and services for office use. These lines have subsequently been reduced in price in order to reduce stock levels.

The location

The shop is situated in a very busy area of the city with a large volume of pedestrians passing the premises. The shop is surrounded by commercial premises and is ideally situated to service local small businesses. However, local business forms only a small proportion of the turnover.

Shop layout

The shop front is very bland and it is not obvious what goods and services are available inside the shop. Once inside the general impression is that of a corner shop, ie disorganised, with goods poorly displayed. Signs displaying the services offered by the shop are well above head height and so many customers will not be fully aware of what is on offer. The area housing the copiers is untidy and is more reminiscent of a printing factory than a retail outlet.

Customers

Steinman Print had not conducted any form of customer analysis itself but the consultants analysed the shop's purchase ledger and found the following.

One customer, GDD, accounted for nearly 10% of the shop's turnover in most months. GDD is one of the factory's main customers. If GDD has any short run work the factory sends it to the shop who will then invoice GDD itself. Other short run work is carried out at the shop for some of the factory's customers. Many customers with credit terms had inactive accounts (no explanation was offered for this).

Sixty per cent of turnover was cash sales (it is assumed that these were individuals making personal purchases rather than business customers). Cash sales were not evenly distributed across the product mix, however, as shown in the table below (these are approximations).

	Copying	Printing	Stationery	Artwork	Total %
% Cash sales	45	35	90	75	60
% Credit sales	55	65	10	25	40

Staffing

There are five staff working in the shop and Ruby who works part-time (2–3 days per week).

James, the manager, is capable of performing any of the functions in the shop and therefore is very useful at 'filling in' if anyone is ill, on holiday or particularly busy. However, he has little organisational ability and has failed to instigate information and control systems which may identify or remove areas of weakness in the current operation.

The printer is occupied most of the day and seems proficient at his job.

Bryan, who is responsible for bulk copying, is not fully utilised in this capacity but when he is unoccupied with copying he serves at the till.

Jill, who serves at the till, is to be made redundant. This seems reasonable as much of the time she is idle. It is anticipated that Ruby and Bryan will be able to carry out the duties which she presently performs.

The artwork illustrators and typesetters, of which there are two, are seriously underworked. However, Joshua believes that it is necessary to provide an artwork/typesetting facility as this work results in printing jobs.

Prices

Stationery items are generally priced with a 50 per cent mark up on cost although for greetings cards the mark up is 100 per cent. The pricing structure for photocopying and printing has not been revised since the shop was taken over. Consequently no one is aware of the rationale behind the pricing policy. In the table below an example of the pricing structure is given.

Number of copies	1	10	100	200	500	1000
A4 copying	0.11	1.05	9.00	17.00	40.00	65.00
A4 printing	N/A	N/A	4.00	6.00	8.00	12.00

For printing jobs a standing charge of £15 is made irrespective of the number of copies.

Costing

No attempt has been made by Steinman Print to analyse the costs involved in photocopying or printing. Also it has no information on the numbers of copies actually made nor the prices at which they had been charged (ie which price breaks were applicable). As A4 copying was perceived to be by far the largest volume of work in these areas the consultants thought it was necessary to try and conduct some form of analysis of the costs involved in this. The information they managed to collate is given below (the consultants were aware that some of the assumptions they made were open to debate but in the absence of primary data these were considered adequate).

Phototcopying (A4 only)

Average monthly sales	£6,400
(figures from the sales ledger where photocopy sales are isolated)	
Paper costs per sheet	0.335p
Toner and cartridge costs per month	£140
(figure derived from the purchases of these items over the period which was then converted to an average charge per month)	
Average number of copies made per month	74,000
(calculated from the photocopier readings made on invoices from the company leasing the equipment)	
Copy charge (per copy)	0.8p
(the leasing company makes a charge of 0.8p per copy made on their equipment. However, each quarter 100,000 copies can be made free of the copy charge)	
Lease charges per month	£2,700
Monthly wages of employee responsible for photocopying	£780

Monthly turnover

Month	Turnover	Month	Turnover
June 1990	27,346	Dec. 1990	22,056
July 1990	26,802	Jan. 1991	27,836
Aug. 1990	23,111	Feb. 1991	25,526
Sept. 1990	28,866	March 1991	25,717
Oct. 1990	27,181	April 1991	23,995
Nov. 1990	26,348	May 1991	27,224

Profit and loss per quarter

	1.6.90– 31.8.90	1.9.90– 30.11.90	1.12.90– 28.2.91	1.3.91– 31.5.91
Sales	77,259	82,395	75,418	76,936
Purchases	24,507	26,572	29,655	24,309
Wages	20,833	20,833	20,833	20,833
Expenses				
Rent, rates, service	13,097	13,097	13,097	13,097
Bank charges/interest	7,000	7,000	7,000	7,000
Leases on equipment	14,607	14,607	14,607	14,607
Copy charges	1,580	1,889	1,281	1,610
Light, heat and power	402	616	650	590
Telephone	1,575	821	853	1,066
Travel	133	131	444	596
Sundries	560	623	732	769
Total purchases, wages and expenses	84,294	86,189	89,152	84,477
Profit (loss)	(7,035)	(3,794)	(13,734)	(7,541)
Cumulative profit (loss)	(7,035)	(10,829)	(24,563)	(32,104)

9 · Medway Menswear Ltd

Bill Richardson and Mary Klemm

Extracts from tape recording of interview between Derek Armitage, managing director of Medway Menswear and Polytechnic consultants.

'The best time to change is when you are doing well! The best time to spend money on changing is when you've got some. If you wait until you are forced to change it's often already too late. It nearly was too late for us, but I think we've managed to turn the tide.'

Derek Armitage got up from his chair, and tidied the papers on his desk.

'Our present position owes much to hard work, effort and co-operation on everybody's part – directors, management and staff throughout the organisation. I'm also aware, however, that we've been lucky. We were in the right place at the right time – as much by chance as by design – and we've picked up two significant customers in the past eighteen months. Without them we'd have been sunk. Also, you know we've had to take some drastic steps on our production side recently. One-third of our factory staff has had to go.

'I don't want to have to go through the traumas of the past couple of years again. What I really need is some advice on how to tackle the future, how to become more efficient, tougher. Perhaps if I show you around the place and give you some facts and thoughts on Medway Menswear Ltd it will be a useful starting point for you. Let's start at the central office. While we're on the way I'll give you the basic information on our organisation, products and customers.

'The business was formed back in the 1920s by my grandfather who started manufacturing industrial clothing from very small premises on this site. From very small beginnings we're now proud of the fact that we are one of the biggest private companies in this industry. For some years now our turnover has been around the £8m mark – although the sources of that turnover have changed somewhat.

'Our product lines now comprise suits, jackets and blazers, trousers and coats, overcoats and industrial uniforms. We supply "off the peg", made-to-measure, or via bulk orders, to a variety of customers including high street multiples and independents, mail order organisations and – on the industrial side – health authorities and police departments. In a way, I suppose, our varied customer and product base has been both "saint and sinner" for us. Certainly we've watched many of our long-established more narrowly-based friends in this industry go into liquidation over the past decade. We have, at least, managed to keep going. However, being so varied gives us all sorts of production scheduling problems and generally seems to have left us – so far as production costs are concerned – as a "jack of all trades and master of none".

'The mail order business, for example – trousers and jackets for the catalogues – is probably no longer profitable. The retailers set the prices to which we have to manufacture. They're the bosses in this industry. So far as mail order is concerned, I think our cost structure is now too high for us to manufacture profitably. Having said that, however, I have to admit that we aren't totally sure about the profitability and contribution of our various lines. Year end accounts have made it clear that some of our pricing and costing has been "out of line".

'Of course, profits have only been part of our recent story. During the really lean times, these orders undoubtedly help maintain capacity and reduce overhead deficits. The business seems to become more and more price competitive. I reckon that our prices, in real terms, haven't increased in the past four years. It's so different to the days of 15 years ago when people were taking all we could make. Of course, we can look back now over the past 15 years and realise the massive effect changing fashion has had on our business. Did you know, for example, that sales of men suits in the UK dropped from 10 million in 1970 to 4 million by 1980. During that period, of course, we were coming to terms with the increasing threat of foreign imports – always substantially cheaper than our offer and in the case of the East Europeans, often of pretty good quality too...

'This is the central office. They look after the accounts, personnel records and customer orders in here. As you can see a lot of our office functions have been computerised recently – some government grants were much appreciated. Computerisation has helped tremendously with credit control and cash flow – a major problem for us. Thirty years ago I seem to remember we never even required bank overdraft facilities. During the past few years we've tended to strain our overdraft limits persistently and we've used leasing facilities for our vehicles to help ease the liquidity situation. We guess that we could improve this position if we went public. Further share issues would also improve our gearing position. However, we're proud of our "private" success and the directors and management want the organisation to maintain its present control structure...

'Despatch, of course, handles the loading of the finished garments into our vans for distribution. These days it's much more a case of filling one van for one destination and one customer. The days when the van visits a number of independent high street retailers with a load of smallish orders have dwindled. It's a reflection of our changing customer base which in turn is a reflection of what's happening on the high street.

'The department also receives raw materials – our basic cloths. They're waiting for a delivery now – cloth which is holding up production. It should have arrived a week ago. Suppliers are another difficulty. There aren't too many British cloth manufacturers left and the ones that are still producing aren't always as responsive to our needs as we'd like. I suppose if we were bigger, or if we could shop around a bit more the 'bargaining' relationship might change...

'The stock room these days is largely a sorting and clearinghouse sitting between the factory and dispatch. Customers used to visit us personally, select garments from the rails and take them away there and then. Again, this has changed. What you see on the rails here are mostly highly standardised garments waiting for the necessary requisition from our large retailer/mail order customers. Not so many years ago 40 per cent of this stock would have been made-to-measure orders – thousands of customised "personally tailored" suits and jackets. This type of business now represents only 3–4 per cent of our turnover – but we'd like to build this up a little because, provided we can meet the quality requirements in the "make" and avoid getting into a series of returns for alteration, this type of business makes us three times the profit earned from our standard "mass products".

'The top sector of the stock room is reserved for Bilton's garments. We're quite excited about our new venture with Bilton. It's a new departure for us – getting into retailing after more than a half century as a menswear manufacturer but, as you know, we now hold a "shop within shops" franchise in 27 of Bilton's South of England stores. Even though they take a hefty chunk of the retail "mark up" it still leaves us with a bigger margin than we're used to getting as simple manufacturers. Of course, what we have to do to take advantage of this opportunity is to sell as many of our garments as we can – and to produce and distribute them efficiently. Things look promising at the moment – in fact I think this venture has played a big role in our survival. However, we are very much still "learners" at this retail game. For example, we are targeting our garments at the 18–40 year old man, but to be honest, we aren't really sure what he's wearing, suit, jacket or trouser-wise, these days. Certainly our traditional view of quality with great attention to the make – things like an extra yoke or double lining – seems to be outdated. We take suggestions from Bilton itself about design and slowly we're learning what sells.

'Presently our franchise outlets are staffed by Bilton's people although we can, if we wish, introduce our own people. I do worry about the motivation of *their* staff towards selling *our* products and I think communications over things such as market and customer requirements could be improved.

'For almost 30 years now we have sold a range of our garments under the brand name of "tailor made". These brand garments have always been promoted as good quality, slightly up-market products and I think that, generally speaking, we have the production capability to do justice to this image. "Tailor made" garments are at the heart of our Bilton franchise. However, I'm a bit worried about the brand name itself. Isn't "tailor made" a little old fashioned? Also one of our sales representatives was telling me last month how a customer had remarked that he had initially thought the brand name to have a Taiwanese "ring" to it.

'We undoubtedly also have many operational improvements to make within our Bilton operation. One aspect that I should appreciate early advice on is that of stock control. You can see, for example, that we are holding thousands of pairs of trousers in the Bilton section of the stock department – I guess there must be around 16,000 garments hanging there now. I'm sure we could save money in the stockholding area – without, of course, jeopardising our overall sales position or, indeed, our relationship with Bilton.

'I'd better explain at this point, however, that the Bilton production set-up is a bit special. You know that we have recently cut back on our production capability. One way we've been able to do this and still maintain turnover is to contract out some of our work. In fact all the trouser production for the Bilton franchise is handled for us by Robert Hunt & Co Ltd – they're an old-established specialist trouser manufacturer based in Lancashire.

'I have some figures here which you might like to play around with, please. Let's see:

- We sold 81,000 pairs of trousers through Bilton's shops last year – at a fairly constant rate.
- Robert Hunt charges £5 per trouser.
- We estimate that our holding costs are about £10 per every 100 pairs of trousers.
- Re-ordering costs work out at about £50 each time. Although orders above 9,000 pairs (the maximum van capacity) incur additional charges of £40 per additional van journey.
- We wait on average, 20–30 days from order to delivery.

'Robert Hunt wrote to me last week saying it was prepared to offer us a 2 per cent discount if we would agree to standardise the relationship into six deliveries per year...

'... We can have an uncluttered view of the production machinery here, at this time. It is, in the main, fairly old. We've computerised the office as you have seen, but the cost of making wholesale technological change in the production department, compared to the benefits and the payback period involved, is too high. We make improvements bit by bit as we can.

'Compared to competition which is able, and willing, to build factories in cheap labour countries, write off investment in tax relief and then move on when the country becomes less amenable, we are obviously at some disadvantage. While this is a problem area, I have to say that in my opinion this industry will remain labour intensive for some years to come.

'We also have an investment choice "on the boil". Jacket sewing, cutting and pressing equipment needs renewing and we're wondering which way to go. Using the present machinery and systems we reckon that our jacket line produces net profit of 6 per cent pa. Jacket production is expected to hold steady at its present level of 100,000 garments per annum, for a number of years to come. Average jacket price is £15.

'We can replace it, from Honers Ltd, with identical equipment which will cost £250,000. A newer machinery supplier – Iztal (UK) Ltd – has also offered us a deal and will supply its equipment at a cost of £300,000. We believe that

Iztal equipment will cut labour and energy costs and we'd expect these savings to increase our net profit margin by 1 per cent to 7 per cent.

'Both suppliers guarantee a six-year life for their products. Of course, you know that cash flow is tight. We'd have to borrow from the bank to finance the investment. The bank will want its "pound of flesh" – 16 per cent per annum at the moment.

'With which firm should we place the contract for the replacement machinery?

'I suppose this is where the "bread is earned" – in the factory. We have 120 girls here, usually, average age of about 19 years. Few seem to stay long after they get married. The maternity provision of a few years ago – the Employment Act, wasn't it? – worried us at the time – we've so many girls of the 'right' age – but in the event I think we've come to terms with its effects.

'Absenteeism is running at 10 per cent which means we must maintain a reserve pool of machinists and our own small training school. Our girls come to be trained on leaving school at 16 – the usual pattern is for them to stay until they start their families, but very few return afterwards. We have been wondering about a job sharing scheme to attract back mature skilled workers – there is a lot of loyalty to the firm in this area. Probably this would reduce absenteeism, but would the savings be swallowed up by extra personnel administration?

'We have briefly considered the issues of multi-skilling and/or group working but decided to stay with job specialisation. Fortunately, we've arrived at tea break time. It's much noisier when everything and everybody is working – and work they must. Productivity is essential. The girls start at 8.30 am and finish at 4.30 pm. In between they have one morning tea break of 15 minutes and a lunch break of 40 minutes. Other than for these "rest periods" it's "heads down". Every making and trimming operation has been "work studied" so that no girl has an operation which lasts more than two minutes. An important part of the process arrives at the end when each girl drops a card into her basket and so records further points towards her piece rate bonus. It's hard work but I hope, and think, that they are a very happy bunch. I like to think "Medway" is a family to *all* who work here and a close friend of the local community.

'Certainly, we have few union problems and, as managing director of an organisation which has pulled itself through some very difficult times, largely because its people have accepted changes and pulled together, I feel a strong obligation towards protecting the future of Medway Menswear Ltd and its people....'

Appendix 9.1 (a) *Medway case study*

Present value factors – interest rates (1% to 14%)

Years	1%	2%	3%	4%	5%	6%	7%	8%	9%	10%	11%	12%	13%	14%
1	.9901	.9804	.9707	.9615	.9524	.9434	.9346	.9259	.9174	.9091	.9009	.8929	.8850	.8772
2	.9803	.9612	.9426	.9246	.9070	.8900	.8734	.8573	.8417	.8264	.8116	.7972	.7831	.7695
3	.9706	.9423	.9151	.8890	.8638	.8396	.8163	.7938	.7722	.7513	.7312	.7118	.6931	.6750
4	.9610	.9238	.8885	.8548	.8227	.7921	.7629	.7350	.7084	.6830	.6587	.6355	.6133	.5921
5	.9515	.9057	.8626	.8219	.7835	.7473	.7130	.6806	.6499	.6209	.5935	.5674	.5428	.5194
6	.9420	.8880	.8375	.7903	.7462	.7050	.6663	.6302	.5963	.5645	.5346	.5066	.4803	.4556
7	.9327	.8706	.8131	.7599	.7107	.6651	.6227	.5835	.5470	.5132	.4817	.4523	.4251	.3996
8	.9235	.8535	.7894	.7307	.6768	.6274	.5820	.5403	.5019	.4665	.4339	.4039	.3762	.3506
9	.9143	.8368	.7664	.7026	.6446	.5919	.5439	.5002	.4604	.4241	.3909	.3606	.3329	.3075
10	.9053	.8203	.7441	.6756	.6139	.5584	.5083	.4632	.4224	.3855	.3522	.3220	.2946	.2679
11	.8963	.8043	.7224	.6496	.5847	.5268	.4751	.4289	.3875	.3505	.3173	.2875	.2607	.2366
12	.8874	.7885	.7014	.6246	.5568	.4970	.4440	.3971	.3555	.3186	.2855	.2567	.2307	.2076
13	.8787	.7730	.6810	.6006	.5303	.4688	.4150	.3677	.3262	.2897	.2575	.2292	.2042	.1821
14	.8700	.7579	.6611	.5775	.5051	.4423	.3878	.3405	.2992	.2633	.2320	.2046	.1807	.1597
15	.8613	.7430	.6419	.5553	.4810	.4173	.3624	.3152	.2745	.2394	.2090	.1827	.1599	.1401
16	.8528	.7284	.6232	.5339	.4581	.3936	.3387	.2919	.2519	.2176	.1883	.1631	.1415	.1229
17	.8444	.7412	.6050	.5134	.4363	.3714	.3166	.2703	.2311	.1978	.1696	.1456	.1252	.1078
18	.8360	.7002	.5874	.4936	.4155	.3503	.2959	.2502	.2120	.1799	.1528	.1300	.1108	.0946
19	.8277	.6864	.5703	.4746	.3957	.3305	.2765	.2317	.1945	.1635	.1377	.1161	.0981	.0829
20	.8195	.6730	.5537	.4564	.3769	.3118	.2584	.2145	.1784	.1486	.1240	.1037	.0868	.0728

Appendix 9.1 (b)

Present value factors – interest rates (15% to 50%)

Years	15%	16%	17%	18%	19%	20%	25%	30%	35%	40%	45%	50%
1	.8696	.8621	.8547	.8475	.8403	.8333	.8000	.7692	.7407	.7143	.6897	.6667
2	.7561	.7432	.7305	.7182	.7062	.6944	.6400	.5917	.5487	.5102	.4756	.4444
3	.6575	.6407	.6244	.6086	.5934	.5787	.5120	.4552	.4064	.3644	.3280	.2963
4	.5718	.5523	.5337	.5158	.4987	.4823	.4096	.3501	.3011	.2603	.2262	.1975
5	.4972	.4761	.4561	.4371	.4190	.4019	.3277	.2693	.2230	.1859	.1560	.1317
6	.4323	.4104	.3898	.3704	.3521	.3349	.2621	.2072	.1652	.1328	.1076	.0878
7	.3759	.3538	.3332	.3139	.2959	.2791	.2097	.1594	.1224	.0949	.0742	.0585
8	.3269	.3050	.2848	.2660	.2487	.2326	.1678	.1226	.0906	.0678	.0512	.0390
9	.2843	.2630	.2434	.2255	.2090	.1938	.1342	.0943	.0671	.0484	.0353	.0260
10	.2472	.2267	.2080	.1911	.1756	.1615	.1074	.0725	.0497	.0346	.0243	.0173
11	.2149	.1954	.1778	.1619	.1476	.1346	.0859	.0558	.0368	.0247	.0168	.0116
12	.1869	.1685	.1520	.1372	.1240	.1122	.0687	.0429	.0273	.0176	.0116	.0077
13	.1625	.1452	.1299	.1163	.1042	.0935	.0550	.0330	.0202	.0126	.0080	.0051
14	.1413	.1252	.1110	.0985	.0876	.0779	.0440	.0254	.0150	.0090	.0055	.0034
15	.1229	.1079	.0949	.0835	.0736	.0649	.0352	.0195	.0111	.0064	.0038	.0023
16	.1069	.0930	.0811	.0708	.0618	.0541	.0281	.0150	.0082	.0046	.0026	.0015
17	.0929	.0802	.0693	.0600	.0520	.0451	.0225	.0116	.0061	.0033	.0018	.0010
18	.0808	.0691	.0592	.0508	.0437	.0376	.0180	.0089	.0045	.0023	.0012	.0007
19	.0703	.0596	.0506	.0431	.0367	.0313	.0144	.0068	.0033	.0017	.0009	.0005
20	.0611	.0514	.0433	.0365	.0308	.0261	.0115	.0053	.0025	.0012	.0006	.0003

10 · M&M Supplies Ltd

Bill Richardson

M&M Supplies Ltd has traded successfully for some years as a manufacturer supplying a variety of retail shops, cafes and restaurants, with its range of meat pies.

Recently M&M has been undertaking market research into the viability of some related diversification – the manufacture of a new prepacked, dehydrated, dog food product. Initial research results have been good and using a prototype machine set up to fill bags to a weight of 500 grams each, 200 sample bags have been produced for use by the company's sales representatives.

However, a chance reference to the new product during a conversation with the company's solicitor culminated in Jane Chadwick, M&M's managing director, seeking advice from the local Weights and Measures Department. The inspector who subsequently called explained that the Weights and Measures Act 1979 applies legal controls to the weights of prepacked goods, and that for prepacked products bearing a marked weight of 500 grams (as per the new M&M product) the following legal rules apply:

1   The average of all such products produced should at least equal the marked weight.
2   Not more than 2.5 per cent of the packages produced should weigh less than 485 grams.
3   No package should weigh less than 470 grams.

The inspector reminded Mrs Chadwick that prosecutions were likely in cases where contraventions of the Act were discovered. He also took the opportunity of reminding Mrs Chadwick that the Food and Drugs Act 1955 might have relevance to the composition of M&M's traditional products (eg pork pies must contain at least 55 per cent pork).

The inspector's visit had left Mrs Chadwick feeling decidedly uncomfortable. She felt that it was likely that the Weights and Measures Department would return at some future time to check the legality of M&M's operations and she was concerned that, despite every wish to operate within the law, poor quality control might cause violations.

Fear of prosecution, and any consequential fine and/or adverse publicity was uppermost in Mrs Chadwick's mind. However, this specific worry had also raised the question of quality control generally. Retail customers had complained over the fluctuating quality of products – in terms of weight, texture and taste. All too often it seemed (on reflection) the end consumer was less than satisfied with M&M's products.

Mrs Chadwick felt that quality failures were due, at least in part, to a mixture of some of the following factors:

- different levels of skill, and care, on the part of production staff (55 people working on a two shift basis) and distribution staff (three van drivers and mates)
- insufficiently 'tight' specifications on baking and machinery processes
- fluctuating quality of ingredients from suppliers.

The week after the inspector's visit, Jane pondered over information provided by a quality control consultant. He had talked of 'assuming a normal distribution' and had promised to return with advice on the legality of the new dog food production process after having worked through the following 'limited sampling statistics'.

Weight of Samples (in grams)
5 consecutive bags taken randomly

Sample numbers	Mean of sample	Range of sample
1–5	500.4	19
6–10	502.2	24
11–15	504.6	11
16–20	498.8	21
21–25	490.6	23
26–30	502.6	17

Jane was also looking at a number of case studies on quality based successful organisations in the 1980s (Pedigree Pet Foods, Jaguar Ltd, Greendale Electronics Ltd) in order to identify how her organisation might improve quality control via the development of a company-wide quality awareness. (See Appendices 10.1–10.3)

Appendix 10.1 *Pedigree Petfoods*

> *'Inspection? That's the last thing we do!'*
> Leslie Simmens
> Managing Director
> Pedigree Petfoods

At Pedigree Petfoods, they believe that everyone is a quality controller – but the last thing they believe in is inspection. 'You can't inspect quality into a product.' They say inspection only weeds out the faults which should never have happened in the first place. It ignores what the customer is getting and concentrates on what he is not getting. It makes you think of quality as a cost, not as a positive value.

At Pedigree, they prefer to put their efforts into 'forward control'. This means operating their plant so mistakes don't happen – or, if they do, are immediately self-evident. It means controlling every ingredient, every process, every machine – systematically, to the precise degree necessary to ensure the desired quality.

The precise dimensions of a can seam are vital to the production process

---

It means training and motivating the workforce to understand that quality control is its main function. It means ensuring that quality is an inevitable attribute at every stage. Inspection for faults comes last – and least.

Don Harrison, production quality superintendent at the Melton Mowbray factory, argues that it is a waste to put your best effort, instruments and skill into inspecting quality at the end of manufacture. These should be part of the manufacturing process.

Responsibility for quality at Pedigree is therefore centred in the production department. Technicians and managers from other departments are involved – including research and process development. Their brief is not so much to eliminate faults as to look for improvements in every part of the manufacturing process.

The biggest section of the production quality department is technical services. They make routine checks on everything from cooling water to the dimension of can seams. They test new products and processes. They identify day-to-day problems – and solve them.

Two smaller sections of PQD study manufacturing methods and quality controls over the longer term.

It's a mathematical, statistical approach, calculating weekly averages and variables, correlating data. Small changes in key figures can give advance notice of major problems in plenty of time to head them off. The system is based on the methods long practised by the parent company, Mars Ltd. The product is different but the principles of quality control are the same.

Sophisticated techniques of statistical analysis ensure that the information extracted from all the figures is itself of high quality and reliability. Too small a sample of production can give a misleading impression, too large a sample is wasteful. With years of experience, PQD have built up a formidable expertise – monitoring every aspect of a complex operation and identifying where to put its efforts and money.

Sterilisation of cans in the factory is, of course, automatically controlled but technical services does a regular double check by attaching a data unit to one of the cans, and sending it all through the process to record times, temperatures and pressures. Afterwards, the data is analysed by computer as part of a continuing process of cross-checks and investigations.

The dimensions of the seam on the ends of cans are also checked regularly by special gauges which feed the measurements into a data bank for analysis and comparison.

Quality control is the main task of everyone who works at Pedigree

---

Samples of finished products are inspected at the end of the process, but that is regarded almost as an afterthought. More significant are the charts on the walls of the panel room where the sampling takes place. These reveal the trends in all the factors that have a bearing on quality.

In this room, there are daily meetings of people from most departments, with marketing, research and production nearly always represented. This is part of another vital aspect of quality control – communication. Facts and ideas are exchanged and discussed. Information is constantly feeding backwards and forwards to and from people for whom quality control is a constant preoccupation.

If new tests and procedures are needed, then full training is given to those who will be responsible for carrying them out. All concerned must understand not only what to do, but why and how. By these methods, quality control becomes more than a practice – it becomes a permanent attitude of mind in everyone working at Pedigree.

The same principles are extended by invincible logic to suppliers.

'We don't spend a lot of time', says Don Harrison, 'inspecting the quality of products coming from suppliers – that would be ridiculous. The cost of quality control is included in what we pay them, so we hold them responsible for their own quality.'

Vendor assurance assessments are carried out by Pedigree on new suppliers, and there is constant contact with old-established suppliers as part of the search for new levels of quality, linked to efficiency and economy.

Quality assurance is a way of life at Pedigree, for everyone. That is easily said, but how is it brought about? How are employees trained and motivated?

Well, in the first place, they don't call them employees – or workers or managers: everyone is an 'associate'. Everyone clocks on, and gets a weekly pay packet or cheque – including the managing director.

A feeling for quality – of decor, environment, comfort, courtesy – is evident in the clean, bright, spacious factory and offices. First names are the rule at and between all levels.

'The quality of our people is the most precious quality of all', says Don Harrison. 'Care is taken over recruiting the best to begin with, and even more effort is put into training and informing them.'

'People must know what is expected of them, what their responsibilities are, where to go if they have a problem', says Don Harrison. 'We have monthly communication meetings to discuss just about everything in the business. We actually stop production to hold them – that's how important it is.'

First-line managers are expected to manage – holding meetings and discussions and presentations as seems necessary in their own areas. Responsibility is exercised at the lowest level in the system that is possible. If an operator on a machine can deal with a fault, he is encouraged to do so. If he needs to refer it to a specialist, he knows to whom to go.

The customers of Pedigree Petfoods do not insist on quality assurance certificates or audits before they buy their tins of Chum, Whiskas or Kit-e-Kat, but they are none the less demanding of quality. They want to be assured of nutritional standards, they want their pet to enjoy the food, they want it to be totally reliable over a period of about 15 years – the normal lifetime of an animal. These are requirements that are more exacting than those for baby foods – or possibly any other canned commodity. Pedigree guarantees that you can feed your pet on its foods exclusively, without incurring any nutritional deficiency; it guarantees they will be packed and presented properly; it guarantees they will be fair value for money.

The final arbiters, of course, are the cats and dogs themselves. They obviously like the stuff. Chum is the leading brand of dog food, and Whiskas is the biggest selling single brand in the grocery business in Britain. The factory at Melton Mowbray is the largest cannery in western Europe, employing 2,000 people. Pedigree must be getting something right.

Appendix 10.2 *Jaguar Cars*

'Our cars had luxury, style, performance – and poor quality!'
'There is no middle ground for Jaguar. We are either among the best in the world – or we just can't exist.'
John L Egan
Chairman
Jaguar Cars

Sometimes a Jaguar arrives at the final vetting point with the label on the indicator stalk scratched. The workers there used to have a simple choice: dismantle the steering column and fit a new indicator stalk – or peel the label off a new stalk from stores and stick it on.

The first remedy involved time, labour and the cost of a new stalk (in total £10–15); the second meant rendering the cannibalised stalk unusable (cost £9). The quality circle suggested that component manufacturers provide a supply of spare stick-on labels. Problem solved: cost – pennies.

There was never anything much wrong with the design or engineering of Jaguar cars. They have always had grace, space, pace – and that touch of magic that fills a man with the desire to possess. So why did Jaguar fail to steal the world market from Mercedes, and BMW? Was it price? No – Jaguars have always cost less than their rivals.

'She's a beauty, and I love her', explained one American devotee, 'but I can't afford a car that lets me down.'

Jaguar's reputation for unreliability was killing a car that all the world wanted to love – that, and poor productivity in the Coventry factory.

In 1979 and 1980, the recession was destroying sales in the UK, and unfavourable exchange rates were giving another twist to the downward spiral of export orders (which normally took half of Jaguar's production). The company was heading for extinction.

In April 1980, a new chairman came to Jaguar and marvelled at the extraordinary paradox he found. On the one hand were glowing descriptions of the new XJ6 Series III, from motoring journalists the world over. On the other hand, John Egan found a seemingly endless catalogue of complaints from owners and dealers about failures and breakdowns.

First, he researched the facts. Hundreds of owners of Jaguars and rival cars were contacted and questioned, and their experiences correlated with warranty statistics to find how many fault codes had to be eliminated. The frightening answer was – 150. The next move was to set up a communications system to tell everyone in the company what the problem was and how it was going to be tackled. The slogan of the campaign was 'In pursuit of perfection'.

Managers from different departments were brought together in task forces, which were allocated groups of faults to investigate and cure. The worst 12 problems were given to the board of directors.

One of the first facts to emerge was that 60 per cent of the faults did not originate with Jaguar at all, they were in brought in components. John Egan went straight to the senior management of Jaguar's suppliers – and discovered that many of them were not aware of the shortcomings of their products, and were grateful to be told. Commented one Jaguar executive 'We had lived with some problems for so long that we had adjusted to them'.

'Adjustments' of that sort were now ruthlessly weeded out. Jaguar insisted that all contracting firms should sign an agreement accepting responsibility for warranty costs arising from failures of their components. Jaguar also let it be known that components would be bought abroad, if foreign quality was better.

'All this seemed to concentrate the mind remarkably', says John Egan. But not all the tactics were so abrasive. At the same time suppliers were invited into the Jaguar factory – and in one extreme case a task force was actually led by a director from a component manufacturer.

Suppliers are now regarded as part of the Jaguar team, and are involved in product design at the earliest stages. Their co-operation has turned to enthusiasm. Components are tested by the original manufacturer to Jaguar standards, and audit systems have been set up to ensure the standards are maintained.

Communicating with the workforce was a bigger and more difficult task. Many were bewildered and disgruntled by changes of management and policy, insecurity and frustration. If the new campaign for quality was to succeed, it had to win their hearts and minds.

The campaign began in earnest by inviting all Jaguar's dealers in the UK to the factory to talk with management and shop stewards. The talk was frank and blunt from Jaguar's side:

'Quality is a joke word on the lips of many Jaguar owners through our lack of success in achieving the standards which they and you have every right to expect. You don't need a detailed graph to know that the levels of our sales have fallen drastically, down 50 per cent in 1979, with these sales lost to our competitors. For every customer we lose each week, 21 jobs are put at stake.'

The speaker was Mike Beasley, manufacturing director. A few days later, he stopped the assembly lines, gathered the workers in the canteen and showed them a video recording of the whole conference. This was followed by a briefing session for management, supervisors and shop floor, with questions and answers all in the same down-to-earth vein.

'It was clear from the outset', says John Egan, 'that emphasising quality met with their full approval. They all wanted to win.'

But there was a hard road ahead. Time-honoured practices had to be swept aside to introduce new methods of quality control, and increase productivity. Tighter disciplines were imposed, and the total workforce was to be reduced by 30 per cent at all levels, including supervision, inspection and rectification. At the same time, quality circles were introduced, making groups of workers responsible for monitoring the quality of work coming in and going out of their area. The philosophy had changed from one of inspecting out faults to one of building in quality.

'The consequences of this programme were quite dramatic', says John Egan. 'We believe that the 50 per cent sales growth we achieved in the US during 1981 was directly attributable to improved quality. We now have over 60 quality circles, involving 10 per cent of our workforce. We would like to have more but we are having to reorganise our management structure to cope with the enormous enthusiasm and request for change required from these active trouble-shooting groups.'

The 'right first time' approach has made everything more predictable. In 1981 and 1982, model launches and production of new models began on time: 95 per cent of total production is now on time.

In 1980, 10,500 workers made 14,105 cars.

In 1982, 7,400 workers made 22,046 cars.

In 1980, the average was 1.34 cars per man; in 1982 this had more than doubled to three cars per man.

Many of the emergency measures of 1980 have now been absorbed into regular custom and practice. Jaguar now telephones directly 150 new owners in Britain and the United States, one month after purchase, and again eight months later. That feedback is passed on to the shop floor by regular video reports on Jaguar's progress.

A note of optimism is now softening the hard-hitting style of those reports. American dealers came to visit the plant, and were interviewed. Said one: 'We have noticed a tremendous improvement in the quality of the vehicles we have received.' Said another: 'We can light the wick on the rocket now, and Jaguar can do more business in the States than ever in their whole history.'

The figures for 1982 proved him right. Sales in the USA were up 120 per cent, and in the UK Jaguar sold more cars then the combined total of all its competitors in the luxury saloon sector. From 1982 to the end of the 1980s the company has wrestled with another problem: it cannot make enough cars to satisfy the demand.

Appendix 10.3 *Greendale Electronics*

> *We have deliberately gone into high-technology areas, because they are not so price-sensitive. We are not competing with Malaysia and Taiwan.'*
> Colin Wemyss
> Managing Director
> Greendale Electronics, Sheffield

Like all firms with a quality assurance system, Greendale Electronics looks hard at the quality systems of its suppliers; and it is choosy about its customers' quality too – even if it means declining to supply them.

In today's world, that is not an easy rule to apply. The reason for it is that Greendale does not make a complete end product, like a car or a television set; its products are components for other people's machines and systems, in telecommunications, power supplies, computer terminals and vehicle test instruments. It would be bad for Greendale's reputation to be associated with a poor quality end product and it would be even worse if the company had to conform to poor design and specifications, forced on it by a customer with third-rate standards.

How does managing director Colin Wemyss handle these difficult and sometimes embarrassing situations?

'With difficulty', he grins, but the fact is that his company can now afford to take that sort of attitude when necessary – indeed, it cannot afford not to. It is now planning to manufacture electronic components for medical instruments, where the safe margin of error is nil, and he does not believe that you can run a factory to varying standards of quality.

The kind of competition that gets the rough edge of Colin Wemyss' Scots tongue is the electronic companies that have mushroomed in recent years, and have often taken Government money without having any solid expertise behind their wares. 'We have been asked to make components to faulty designs and poor specifications, and we have had to refuse to do it', he says.

What makes him even angrier are customers who take his designs and hand them over to be made on the cheap by just such companies. 'In the end, there is only one answer', he says, 'and that is quality. That is where we defeat them.'

The success of Greendale's quality policy speaks for itself. When Crystalate

Holdings, the parent company, bought Greendale five years ago, the net assets of the company were £23,000: today, they are £538,000. Crystalate's shares have gone from 5p to £1.65 over the same period.

Before the takeover, Greendale was a medium-to-low technology company making equipment mainly for the Post Office. A downturn in orders had reduced it to making camp stools, just to keep the employees in work. Crystalate bought the company for the sake of the undeveloped skills within it, and as a vehicle for its ambitions in the electronics field. The policy was to sell into the high added-value, high technology markets, and to phase out low-profit, high-volume products. A massive investment plan of half a million pounds was started. BS 9000 approval was obtained for telecommunication products for British Telecom, with a quality management system to BS 5750.

On these standards and their application, Colin Wemyss is quite inflexible, but the rest of his management style is relaxed and open. He believes that his management committee should run the company day to day, and that everyone should be free to question working practices. He sees no virtue in hierarchies or deference.

A monthly works council is the principal means of communication with the workforce, with day-to-day news passed on by supervisors. 'If we are losing money one month', he says, 'we tell them, if we have a success we make sure they know.' But he admits that management–worker relations have not yet progressed as far as he would like. As a Scot, accustomed to working with American multinationals in the past, often with entirely new factories in new industries, he has always been used to an egalitarian, collaborative relationship from shop floor to board room. The dour scepticism of South Yorkshire came as a toe-stubbing surprise.

Traceability of worker as well as of materials, for example, is an essential part of a quality assurance system, but he encountered resistance from the operatives because they saw it as a threat. Colin Wemyss wants them to see it as a way of identifying problems of technique, so that help and training can be given where they are needed.

He recognises that many of the reactions are born of historic experience in older industries, with authoritarian management, and that human attitudes cannot be changed overnight. He believes that bonus and productivity schemes, share options and constant communication will win hearts and minds. Already, there are signs of change. A scheme for self-certification in illness was introduced, and was followed by a marked fall in absenteeism. Two quality circles have been started, and are beginning to discover for themselves their own scope and purpose.

So far, quality assurance systems at Greendale have reduced the proportion of rejects (which are largely worthless in electronics) from 28 per cent to 4 per cent. With 100,000 units of production a year, at an average cost of £10.80 per unit, it adds up to a saving of around a quarter of a million pounds. That figure feeds through almost entirely into profits.

One of the quality circles is on the production line making VDU terminals for IBM, a company that can be unforgiving of repeated quality faults, but keenly appreciative of quality improvement. Colin Wemyss and Greendale are proud to have IBM's seal of approval. They are even prouder of the accolade they received this year – Greendale are to make a unit for a major electronics manufacturer which will go directly to its customers, without inspection by the firm concerned.

That is the meaning of quality assurance.

Section 4 · Public sector organisations

11 · Rutshire County Council Consumer Protection Department

Bill Richardson

This case study has been written by Bill Richardson from general experience. It is intended to be used as the basis for class discussion rather than as a comment on the handling of a business situation.

In 1982 Fred Hartley looked back with some pride – and some regret – over his career.

As Chief Officer of Rutshire County Council's Consumer Protection Department since local government reorganisation in 1974 Fred had been responsible for the integration of the old Weights and Measures Departments of the four major towns in Rutshire (Malchester, Ronfield, Drayton and Cranthorpe) and the subsequent operation of the county-wide service.

Not surprisingly the county structure had been headed by 'Weights and Measures men' most of whom Fred knew as Malchester colleagues or members of the 'tightly-knit' Institute of Trading Standards Administration. The identities of the former local town services had been maintained via the creation of town-based divisions organised on a functional basis and linked to a new, centrally situated, Head Office at Dortown. Appendix 11.1 gives details in the form of an organisation chart.

In the mould of its mother organisation (Rutshire County Council) the Department was based on clear hierarchies of seniority and communication links and voluminous rules and job descriptions. Such structural characteristics remained fundamental (and became a focal point in any disputes) although a less formal structure exhibiting much lateral communication and discretion as to which jobs to tackle and how to perform them had also evolved. Divisional staff worked closely together in the same premises and through the facility of 'car user allowance' were highly mobile across divisions. Quick meetings, discussions during chance meetings and telephone conversations were preferred to more formal lines and methods of communication. The nature of many of the working problems faced by field staff demanded initiative, speed and flexibility. Appendix 11.2 illustrates some of the areas of operation.

The first four years of the new Department had been almost idyllic. NALGO (National and Local Government Officers' Association) was strong but not particularly militant. Job security was high – nobody ever 'got the sack' from Rutshire. Staff control, potentially difficult given the history and nature of many of the people employed and the jobs to be done had never been a problem. The predominantly young people of the Department (average age in 1975 had been less than 30) had emerged from their Weights and Measures localised environments into a wider and better resourced consumer protection operation. Most received some form of promotion and/or salary increase and many (particularly those who were redeployed in the consumer affairs section) found the newer areas of consumerism (eg trade descriptions, consumer credit, consumer advice, research and publicity) stimulating. New staff recruited from business and higher education for the skills and experience they could bring to these newer functions were also keen to do a good job and happy to be in 'the sort of occupation which gives you a worthwhile job and lets you get on with doing it'.

The later years of Fred's 'reign', however, were characterised by growing 'rumblings' of disquiet.

While 1974's reorganisation had produced a very attractive package of benefits for everyone nothing much had improved since then. The Department was generally recognised as being the poor relation in comparison to major county functions such as Highways and Environment and with central sources of funds becoming increasingly scant the early euphoria of growth and development was soon curtailed.

Staff morale was also affected by increasing workloads. As advice/complaint enquiries rose from levels of 22,000 per year to 40,000 per year staff involved in these areas began to resent 'having too much of the same thing to do'. New pieces of consumer legislation introduced in the 1970s and early 1980s – without any accompanying additional resources – added to the Department's already extensive catalogue of legislative obligations and duties. Staff complained about the lack of policy direction on the issue of which of the competing work objectives of quality and quantity should be given priority. They remained suspicious, too, about the computerised record-keeping system which emphasised, in statistical form, the volume of work performed.

Further, Fred had noted a growing resentment from the non-Weights and Measures sections of his staff about the traditional practice which precluded anyone other than a Weights and Measures qualified person from obtaining a managerial position in the organisation. Appendix 11.3 gives some information on the types of people employed in different sections of the Department.

Non-'ticket' holders, particularly from the consumer affairs section, were voicing their resentment of their perceived 'second class' status. Certainly job turnover was highest in this section although this was variously ascribed to a number of factors including the following:

- the training nature and qualifications of these personnel made the securing of outside occupations more natural and easy
- motherhood (a significant proportion of the section was female)
- the desire to leave what might otherwise be a long-term career because of the lack of advancement opportunities.

Managers involved in selection procedures maintained that the promotion/advancement situation had been covered in selection interviews although this assertion was disputed by some 'non-qualified' staff members.

Generally, staff morale was reducing.

Matters became particularly tense over issues of accountability when staff objected to a directive insisting on better record-keeping. Accusations of a broken promise that the recent introduction of computerised record-keeping would not lead to computer statistics being used for individual appraisal and control purposes were levied at Fred personally. A dispute over job descriptions and short manning led to his handing in his NALGO 'hat' to concentrate more clearly on his managerial function. In 1982, with some misgivings, the 'wise old owl' of Rutshire's Consumer Protection Department took early retirement.

The new regime

Charles Crawley was in his early 40s, ambitious, bright and hard working. His professional career had been spent in local authority trading standards enforcement work. Weights and Measures qualified and a member of the Institute of Trading Standards Administration, Charles' appointment to the position of chief officer of Rutshire's Consumer Protection Department provided him with experience of a third local authority system.

Some of the internal, defeated candidates were openly disparaging of his more aggressive approach and of his 'careerist' route to the top of consumer protection ('moving loyalties to get twice as far in half the time'). His ambition and dynamism, however, was seen as appropriate to the more positive presentation of the Department's public face during a period when the County Council itself was engaged in a campaign against the Government's plans to abolish the metropolitan county councils.

Charles acknowledged the wealth of resources and reputation which had been developed by Rutshire's Consumer Protection Department over the years and looked forward to developing these aspects further. He immediately set about the task of creating 'his team'. Very astutely, according to some observers, he selected an 'inner circle' of about ten people (all Weights and Measures men with the exception of the home economist). These people were drawn away from their traditional duties and spent increasing proportions of their time working from Head Office. Much emphasis was placed on showing a public face and on finding newsworthy situations to report. To many it now seemed that someone from the 'upper echelon' was always on local TV, radio or in the newspapers. Further forays by Charles to the extremes of his organisation brought in other officers for the purpose of developing 'projects'. These changes were made quickly and informally. Attempts to attain a useful and formally recognised new structure, however, were consistently resisted by union representatives and by the staff in free votes on proposed changes.

A new sense of vibrancy permeated the organisation. Its external face was one of proactivity, professionalism and concern for the consumer. Internally, the status of officers now depended upon their closeness to Charles and their associations with the increasingly important functions of publicity and projects. Traditional duties seemed to be taking a back seat.

Most of those 'pulled out' for projects by Charles welcomed their new status and job enrichment. Many left at the periphery of the organisation, however, began to feel resentful. Now even fewer officers were left at divisional level to perform the ongoing, everyday, tasks. Fewer inspections were being carried out – those inspectors left at Divisions refused to cover the areas left by their seconded colleagues. At the advice centres consumer advisers found themselves managing much of the time without their senior advisers in attendance. They also complained about the extra work being generated by the new levels of publicity and of often 'finding out what the Department had said to the media the day before' from the customers coming into the advice centres. They also pointed out the paradox of being left to manage under a system which refused to accept their pertinence as managers. As point of first contact for 95% of the Department's customers they felt angry about being left on the perimeter of the organisation 'to get on with it'.

For the first time in its history the Department's advice centres began closing for lunch. On a couple of occasions, because relief staff from other sections were either unavailable, or unwilling, to cover, the Ronfield centre closed its doors during normal working hours. Previously, flexible cover of this nature had always been available as a matter of course. Many advisers began operating as pure advisers (rather than as assistors/interventionists). Two divisionally-employed Weights and Measures inspectors left Rutshire for similar posts with other authorities.

In 1984 a rare vacancy in the consumer affairs section produced a recruitment advertisement which again restricted the class of applicants to Weights and Measures qualified personnel. A memo expressing concern over the continuation of this 'restrictive practice' signed by 30 staff members drawn from consumer affairs, enforcement and clerical sections was handed to Charles and set in motion a series of meetings between Charles and the departmental representatives over the issue. Subsequently, a new advertisement was published offering the post of Senior Trades Descriptions Officer at Ronfield Division to Weights and Measures qualified applicants *plus* other appropriately qualified/experienced personnel. The post, which had been 'blacked' was opened up and attracted a number of internal applicants. Appendix 11.4(a) provides brief CV details of the applicants (all of whom were interviewed).

John Treeton was offered the job and he accepted. Many of the other candidates referred to the selection process and the interview as 'a joke process'. Generally John's new colleagues were disappointed to find that John spent much of his time on project work for Charles rather than on the traditional aspects of trade descriptions work. Within three months of the appointment Lawrence Hinds had left the Department to work for a national finance company.

Shortly after the Ronfield position had been filled the similar post at Cranthorpe became available. Appendix 11.4(b) gives details of candidates. James Fox was appointed.

Meanwhile, the vacancy created by John Treeton's appointment and transfer also formed the basis of a recruitment and selection procedure. This senior advisory officer post was strongly expected to provide *the* major breakthrough – the appointment of a non-Weights and Measures person to a senior, managerial position. Culturally this post was furthest away from the traditional Weights and Measures bastions of inspection and law enforcement. It was also acknowledged as offering 'some of the hardest work to be had in the Department'. Candidates are considered briefly in Appendix 11.4(c).

Russell Hardcastle was appointed to the post. Within six months Ruth Jones had left to join a business education consultancy firm and William Bright had secured a position as a legal executive with another local authority.

Much time was spent (during working hours) discussing the situation of the non-qualified staff. William summed up the feelings of many of his colleagues. 'This is a good job, basically. We have a free hand, by and large, and you can really do a good job for the people and the community. The problem is, is that the job needs self-motivation and after a while of being treated "second class" you feel it's stupid bothering. Why should we graft when others are assured of the recognition and rewards – particularly when you feel that you're better than them at the job and basically more committed to it?'

A number of 'non-qualified' staff commenced a mass grievance procedure against Charles. Soon after the Cranthorpe senior advisory post was advertised. Only three people applied for the job – all internal candidates and all 'non-qualified' consumer affairs staff.

Roy Dale (formerly the Consumer Credit Officer at Cranthorpe) duly became the first 'non-qualified' manager of the Rutshire Consumer Protection Department. Within a year the entire Department was dismantled and rehoused in various forms in the original Borough Councils of the County. In accord with Government plans Rutshire County Council was abolished in 1986.

Appendix 11.1 *Rutshire County Council Consumer Protection Department organisation structure*

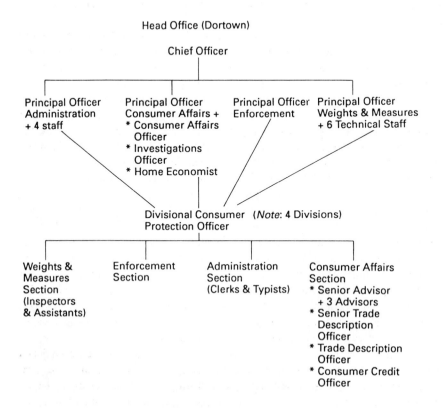

Head Office (Dortown)

Chief Officer

Principal Officer
Administration
+ 4 staff

Principal Officer
Consumer Affairs +
* Consumer Affairs
  Officer
* Investigations
  Officer
* Home Economist

Principal Officer
Enforcement

Principal Officer
Weights & Measures
+ 6 Technical Staff

Divisional Consumer (*Note*: 4 Divisions)
Protection Officer

Weights &
Measures
Section
(Inspectors
& Assistants)

Enforcement
Section

Administration
Section
(Clerks & Typists)

Consumer Affairs
Section
* Senior Advisor
  + 3 Advisors
* Senior Trade
  Description
  Officer
* Trade Description
  Officer
* Consumer Credit
  Officer

Appendix 11.2

PUSHCHAIR SURVEY
Findings Give Cause for Concern
Many parents could be pushing their children
around in faulty or even unsafe pushchairs.
They could also be misusing the pushchair
to the detriment of the child and the pushchair.

You may have heard or read recently that this department intended to carry out pushchair MOTs and understandably wondered what it was all about. Well, it all began when we received a serious complaint about a pushchair which caused a child to loose the ends of two fingers. As a result of this and other complaints about pushchairs, we decided to carry out a modest survey to discover if these complaints were isolated incidents or if there really was cause for concern over the safety, standard and use of pushchairs.

The county-wide checks, which involved examining pushchairs in use and talking to parents, revealed that there is cause for concern. Of all the pushchairs examined (nearly all were the baby-buggy type) 81 per cent were found to be faulty and 25 per cent were declared unfit for use. To make matters worse the majority of these faults were found on pushchairs under 1 year-old and yet most parents expected their pushchairs to last 2–3 years. Faults, however, were not the only problem, there were also many examples of misuse on the owner's part such as heavy shopping bags hanging from the handles causing instability and strain.

The information we have collected obviously points to a need to improve the standard of baby-buggy type pushchairs and so we will be making representations to manufacturers, the British Standard Institution and the Department of Trade. In the meantime, you can read the details of our findings, our comments and advice on pages 2 and 3 and if you are thinking of buying a pushchair, our special Pushchair Price Survey could save you money.

ONE-DAY SALES

In the weeks before Christmas you may well find a leaflet pushed through your letter-box advertising a One-Day Sale in a local pub or church hall. If the leaflet proclaims unbelievable bargains like continental quilts from £2.00, Black and Decker drills from £5.00, toasters from £1.00, be very wary. These bargains sound too good to be true and they usually are as none of the advertised goods are ever offered for sale. 'The van broke down on the way here' is often one of the excuses given for the lack of these advertised goods.

This type of one-day sale should not be confused with the well-established one-day sales which are often held in hotels and are well advertised in the local press. At this type of sale the goods are on display and clearly marked with their price and can be examined. At the type of sale we are warning you about the goods are never on display but placed on a table besides the salesman on the stage.

The salesman, who will tell the audience several times it is a sale, not an auction, will get the attention of the crowd by offering for sale items at much less than they are worth. Unfortunately, having got the audience interested, the salesman will eventually be able to sell them goods which are worth far less than the amount paid. A radio sold for £15 but worth only £5 and a set of crockery also sold for £15 retailing at £4 in a local shop are just two examples of how these fast talking, persuasive salesmen take people for a ride and make a huge profit for themselves.

So if you are tempted to attend one of these sales, do not get carried away by the sales patter and ask yourself if you are really getting a bargain. You can probably buy the same goods more cheaply locally and you will know where to find the seller if you have a complaint.

If you do get a leaflet advertising a one-day sale pushed through your letter-box would you let us know immediately and then one of our officers can attend the sale to see if any offences are committed.

CHRISTMAS IS COMING
Once again we will be carrying out special Christmas Price Surveys to help you save time and money at Christmas.

The first Christmas Price Survey to be published will be on Toys and Games. Although we have carried out this survey for several years the savings to be made by shopping around never fail to amaze us...

IN THIS ISSUE
The consumer information magazine which provides the news, advice and information, enabling you to buy wisely, looks at ...

Bills and Debts
It is so easy for bills to mount up, but what can you do if you are not able to pay them?

Glittering Lamps
Are they a hazard? See our findings.

Cars
Thinking of buying a car this summer? Read our article before you do.

Shoes
'My shoes are killing me' – a familiar cry – our 'Help Yourself' column and 'Mrs Price' provide some useful information on buying shoes.

Miles per Gallon
Did you know there are new regulations in force regarding information about the fuel consumption of cars?

Appendix 11.3 *Rutshire County Council Consumer Protection Department staff profile*

Weights and Measures qualified staff

Approximately 40 of the 120 staff employed by the Department held the Weights and Measures 'ticket' – a qualification with statutory backing and awarded by the Department of Trade. Traditionally the 'ticket' had been associated with the Weights and Measures Act 1963 and the inspectorate duties contained therein. A recent ruling by the Inspectors' Association (ITSA) had insisted that only graduates were eligible to train as Weights and Measures Inspectors (a minimum two years on-the-job/study/exam programme).

All managerial jobs (except those in admin. and personnel) were allocated to Weights and Measures 'ticket holders'. Managers' vacancies were advertised exclusively to those holding the qualification and so ensured a managerial route for those Weights and Measures people currently employed in the traditional role of 'inspectors'. Weights and Measures Inspectors commanded one grade higher on the salary scale premium than other 'field' professionals. Generally, 'ticket holders' were a very tightly-knit group of professionals who sought to maintain the status of their important but occupation-specific qualification.

Weights and Measures Assistants

Traditionally, each Weights and Measures Inspector had an assistant to take the burden of some of the more onerous duties involved in the Weights and Measures function (eg carrying heavy weights, shovelling coal in coal weight checks, etc.). This tradition had been maintained and the Department employed around 20 such staff – 'a silent army'.

Consumer Affairs Staff

Apart from the managerial posts in this section the staff employed came from a variety of backgrounds with a wide range of experience and qualifications (eg MSc, BA, HND, AIB (Associate Institute of Bankers), ACIS (Associate Chartered Institute of Secretaries), teaching certificate). They worked in the newer areas of consumerism from the county's prestigious advice centres performing duties associated with consumer advice, trade descriptions, consumer credit and research/publicity. Such staff were encouraged to study for the Diploma in Consumer Affairs. Rewards for the attainment of such a qualification were for consumer affairs staff, removal of the bar which stopped staff moving up the admin. and professional salary grades and, perhaps into the first tier of the senior salary range.

Three 'non-qualified' consumer affairs staff were employed at Head Office.

Enforcement Officers

The County employed 12 enforcement officers whose jobs were associated with the enforcement of consumer safety and food and drugs legislation. Most of these employees were long service people who had trained as Weights and Measures Inspectors in the days before the graduate entry ruling but who had not attained the 'ticket' qualification.

Clerical and Administration

Headed by a principal officer based at Head Office (holding the Diploma in Public Administration) this section provided back-up support to the 'field' officers.

Appendix 11.4 *Rutshire County Council Consumer Protection Department vacant post candidates*

(a) *Post of Senior Trade Descriptions Officer, Ronfield*

Candidates	*CV Details*
George Hunt	46 years old. Ten years experience at TDO (Trade Descriptions Officer) in Malchester office. No formal qualifications. Useful record in post.
Brian Rogers	41 years old. Originally a Weights and Measures trainee with another local authority but did not obtain 'ticket'. For past ten years worked as TDO in Cranthorpe. Had run this section during past vacancies and had provided induction training for his two previous Senior TDOs. Excellent record in trade description work and well respected by other staff.
Lawrence Hinds	31 years old. Eight years within the Ronfield TD section specialising in consumer credit but doing much TD work also. Useful record of TD investigations and prosecutions. Together with Gary Andrews (see below) had been running the section during the present vacancy of the past six months. AIB + teaching certificate.
William Bright	30 years old. Eight years in Drayton office (four as an adviser, last four as consumer credit officer also working in TD matters). Successful general and TD-related record. BABS(Hons) and Diploma in Consumer Affairs.
Gary Andrews	27 years old. TD Officer for previous ten months in Ronfield. Previously Technical Officer at HO and prior to this sergeant in army.
Andrew Marples	38 years old. Weights and Measures Inspector at Cranthorpe office for past nine years.
John Treeton	Weights and Measures qualified plus DCA. Presently senior consumer adviser at Drayton and a successful record in this post over past ten years. Of late had been spending an increasing amount of time on project work and central publicity. Had liaised with TD section at Drayton but little practical experience in the field and no track record.

(b) *Senior Trade Descriptions Officer, Cranthorpe*

Andrew Marples	(as 4(a))
George Hunt	(as 4(a))
Brian Rogers	(as 4(a))
Gary Andrews	(as 4(a))
David Eccles	32 years old. Past eight years as Weights and Measures Inspector at Drayton.

James Fox   Almost identical to John Treeton but Senior Advisory post at Cranthorpe.

(c) *Senior Advisory Officer, Drayton*

Russell Hardcastle   33 years old. Weights and Measures Inspector for past six years in Malchester office. Had spent approximately half a day per week over past six months helping out in the Malchester advice centre.

William Bright   (as 4(a))

George Anderson   30 years old. Formerly an assistant in Drayton advice centre. Had been a mainstay in the continued operation of Drayton advice centre during recent months. DCA held.

Ruth Jones   28 years old. Past two years as consumer adviser in Cranthorpe. BA.

Alan Fieldman   55 years old. An advisory officer from the pre-1974 days when Malchester had formed the first consumer advice centre in the country. Well-respected and used to managing the busy Malchester centre during the frequent illness-forced absences of the present Malchester senior adviser.

Appendix 11.5 *Rutshire County Council – Revenue Expenditure 1980/81 to 1984/85*

COMMITTEE Gross expenditure	1980/81 (£'000)	%	1981/82 (£'000)	%	1982/83 (£'000)	%	1983/84 (£'000)	%	1984/85 (£'000)	%
Consumer Protection	1,540	1	1,686	1	1,920	1	1,979	1	2,079	1
Environment	6,137	4	5,596	3	6,758	3	6,535	3	7,198	3
Fire service	11,742	7	13,519	7	15,697	6	16,656	7	18,032	6
Highways	43,931	26	49,679	25	56,993	24	57,713	24	59,590	22
Passenger transport	49,033	29	61,780	31	73,825	31	77,265	32	73,595	27
Planning	1,547	1	2,438	1	2,733	1	2,844	1	2,834	1
Less – Recharges	–	–	705Cr	–	799Cr	–	848Cr	–	810Cr	–
Police	43,142	25	50,014	26	57,680	24	63,369	26	94,054	34
Policy										
Central establishment	7,826	4	8,027	4	8,908	4	9,487	4	9,659	3
Less recharges	7,568Cr	4Cr	7,814Cr	4Cr	8,637Cr	4Cr	9,144Cr	4Cr	9,274Cr	3Cr
Probation	3,865	2	4,489	2	5,084	2	5,507	2	6,005	2
Other services	5,542	3	6,516	3	7,400	3	7,604	3	7,856	3
Recreation, culture and health	1,251	1	1,303	1	1,640	1	2,112	1	2,677	1
	167,978	99	196,528	100	229,202	96	241,079	100	273,495	100
Contribution to Capital Fund	2,553	1	–	–	–	–	–	–	–	–
Contribution to Renewal & Repairs Fund	–	–	–	–	10,000	4	–	–	–	–
Provision for bad debts	–	–	–	–	40	–	–	–	–	–
	170,531	100	196,528	100	239,242	100	241,079	100	273,495	100

Appendix 11.5 *continued*

COMMITTEE Gross expenditure	1980/81 (£'000)	%	1981/82 (£'000)	%	1982/83 (£'000)	%	1983/84 (£'000)	%	1984/85 (£'000)	%
Financed from -										
Precept	123,720	72	78,887	40	96,093	40	103,345	43	113,665	42
Government grants	38,485	23	108,420	55	121,885	51	116,278	48	137,384	50
Other income	13,271	8	13,162	7	16,162	7	16,969	7	17,709	7
Contribution from Renewal & Repairs Fund	–	–	–	–	–	–	900	–	3,093	1
Appropriation of DLO Balances	–	–	–	–	–	–	–	–	900	–
Utilisation of miscellaneous receipts	–	–	–	–	–	–	–	–	744	–
Balances	4,945Cr	3Cr	3,941Cr	2Cr	5,102	2	3,587	2	–	–
	170,531	100	196,528	100	239,242	100	241,079	100	273,495	100

Appendix 11.6 *Rutshire County Council – Capital Expenditure 1980/81 to 1984/85*

COMMITTEE	1980/81 (£'000)	%	1981/82 (£'000)	%	1982/83 (£'000)	%	1983/84 (£'000)	%	1984/85 (£'000)	%
Gross expenditure										
Consumer protection	79	1	22	–	72	–	97	1	5	–
Environment	2,055	12	2,246	11	2,301	10	2,879	13	1,684	8
Fire service	95	1	199	1	1,540	6	1,359	6	1,813	9
Highways	8,948	51	11,394	58	11,837	50	11,688	52	13,011	65
Highways – Direct labour organisation	–	–	56	–	643	3	174	1	8	–
Passenger transport	–	–	–	–	200	1	–	1	128	1
Planning	–	–	–	–	–	–	–	–	–	–
Police	2,545	14	3,246	17	3,402	14	2,569	11	1,623	8
Policy										
Central establishment	192	1	478	2	783	3	108	1	107	1
Probation	25	–	21	–	13	–	25	–	164	1
Other services	3,399	19	1,878	10	1,688	7	1,660	7	1,019	5
Recreation, culture and health	89	1	239	1	1,317	6	1,824	8	522	2
	17,427	100	19,779	100	23,796	100	22,383	100	20,084	100
Financed from										
Loan	8,321	48	14,420	73	19,675	83	18,823	84	14,445	72
Government grants	3,252	19	2,273	11	1,303	5	2,987	13	4,645	23
Capital receipts	194	1	146	1	395	2	181	1	324	2
Capital fund	5,467	31	–	–	–	–	–	–	–	–
Revenue	435	2	2,826	14	2,416	10	259	1	69	–
Balances	242Cr	1Cr	114	1	7	–	133	1	601	3
	17,427	100	19,779	100	23,796	100	22,383	100	20,084	100

Appendix 11.7 *Rutshire County Council budget summary 1985/86*

	1985/86 Estimate £'000
NET REQUIREMENTS	
Transportation	
Highways	34,380
Less: Transport	
Supplementary grant	(3,838)
	30,542
Passenger transport	78,050
	108,592
Less: Transport	
Supplementary grant	–
	108,592
Other services	
Consumer protection	1,822
Environment	3,974
Fire service	16,079
Planning	1,737
Police	29,699
Policy	
Probation	1,165
Other services	4,867
Recreation, culture and health	1,880
	61,223

Note: In the face of rate-capping and a 'recalcitrant government' (Leader's Annual Report) 1985/86 was to be a year of financial stringency with the Consumer Protection Department's budget being cut by 10 per cent on 1984/85 levels.

Appendix 11.8 *Rutshire County Council*
Consumer Protection Department budget for 1984/85

£	
£1,750,000	Wages and staff development costs (138 personnel[1])
5,000	Capital expenditure (new Weights and Measures Testing Equipment)
250,000	Rent, rates, heating, lighting and upkeep of premises (4 divisional offices, 4 consumer advice centres, 1 central office)
10,000	'Test' purchases of products and services to ensure legal weights, descriptions, fitness for purpose, etc.
69,000	Miscellaneous purchases, PR, professional advice, etc. £10,000 per division + £19,000 central 'overall' fund
£2,084,000	

Note:[1] 2 Weights and Measures Inspectors, 2 Consumer Advisers, 1 Consumer Credit Officer and 1 Admin Assistant had resigned within the last two months of the year.

Appendix 11.9 *Manpower statement*

The table below shows the overall number of personnel employed on services wholly or partly financed by the County Council on 31 March 1985 as compared to 10 March 1984.

Committee or service	In Post 10.3.84	In Post 31.3.85
Consumer protection		
APT&C[1]	128	122
Manual	10	10
	138	132
Environment		
APT&C	116	118
Manual	146	146
	262	264
Fire service		
Uniformed and retained fireman	1,277	1,267
APT&C	69	66
Manual	111	105
	1,457	1,438
Highways		
APT&C	955	909
Manual	1,210	1,163
	2,165	2,072
Passenger Transport		
SYPTE manual	4,556	4,353
SYPTE non-manual	775	776
	5,331	5,129
Planning and architecture		
APT&C	155	143
Police[2]		
APT&C	471	477
Manual	272	273
School crossing patrols	570	566
	4,239	4,243
Prosecuting solicitors		
APT&C	68	65

Committee or service		In Post 10.3.84	In Post 31.3.85
Policy and other services			
Administration	– APT&C	207	198
	– Manual	94	92
Treasurers	– APT&C	268	243
		569	533
Probation		389	456
Recreation, culture and health			
APT&C		51	56
Manual		28	31
		79	87

Notes: [1] APT&C – Administrative, Professional, Technical and Clerical Staff.
[2] Police uniformed personnel are not employees of the County Council.

12 · Privatisation of hospital laundry

Peter Prowse

Briefing for managers

You have recently been appointed general manager of Knighton Hospital in Yorkshire and have a personnel officer and deputy site manager in your department.

Background

The Authority faces revenue reductions this financial year. A decision has been made by the Authority to review a number of support service departments in order to assess the possibility of contracting out rather than maintaining the services in-house. The potential review departments are transport, laundry, domestic, catering and works.

It is now Government policy that the cost-effectiveness of the National Health Service (NHS) support services, particularly laundry, domestic and catering should be tested with private sector alternatives.

In September 1983 a health circular HC(83)18, was sent to all health authorities. The circular stipulated that the cost-effectiveness of these services should be tested, taking account of the capacity of the commercial contractors to provide services, by putting them out to tender (including in-house tenders).

The problem

The first service to be tested at Knighton was transport. A feasibility study was initiated in January 1990 and by August 1990 the study and tendering process had been completed. The in-house tender was accepted by the District Health Authority (DHA) as the most cost-effective and the decision was implemented in October 1990.

The second feasibility study was carried out on the laundry service. Following the study and a range of tenders from commercial contractors and in-house, the DHA awarded the contract to Advance Linen Services of Pontefract. The formal contract was signed on 26 January 1991.

Prior to the award of the contract to Pontefract the bulk of the laundry from Knighton Hospital had been done at Heeley Laundry, within the NHS but not on site at Knighton. However, there was an element of work, sluicing the foul wash (blood and soiled linen), which was the work of the sewing room department. Following sluicing and re-bagging, the linen was then processed by Heeley Laundry. This work accounted for 44 hours per week and was lost when the contract was awarded to the commercial contractor. The union, GMWU, registered a trade dispute on 1 February 1991 and a request that no changes should be made to the sluice job, ie a request that the status quo be maintained.

You have rejected this request and feel that the contract signed on 21 January must be observed.

The next day you arrive at the hospital to find a picket line of ancillaries at the hospital gates. Your personnel officer reports that 200 out of 300 ancillaries are out on strike over the loss of the post.

YOUR AIM IS TO RESOLVE THE DISPUTE BUT YOU CANNOT RESCIND THE CONTRACT.

13 · Crossed wires at British Telecom

Bill Richardson

This case study is based on research including reference to media articles. It is not intended as a comment on the handling of a business situation but as an aid to class discussion of business policy issues. It provides a 1987 perspective of British Telecom and follows this with information on BTs activities in the early 1990s.

'The span of our activities and services, the technology, the requirements of our customers, the increasing strength and breadth of home competition and the pattern of regulation are, as expected, all moving on', claimed BT chairman, Sir George Jefferson as he announced the 1986 reorganisation of British Telecom. Telecom's UK network operation was to be regrouped into an Inland Communications division and a Business Services division. The Business Services division was to comprise two units – one handling general business networks operations and the other handling the specialist needs of large business customers. The reorganisation also created a new International Products division. The basic organising principles of 'devolved responsibility with accountability' were to continue to underlie the new organisation structure.

One year on from the reorganisation BT's top management could look back on a range of mixed opinions over the level of success the organisation had achieved, since its privatisation, in adapting to its business situation. Mid-1987 seemed like a particularly pertinent time to reflect on the past, look forward to the future and take stock of the present.

In fact, in the space of six turbulent years British Telecom, in a variety of legally constituted forms and under different organisational names, had experienced much change and adaptation. Some important dates and events leading towards a declared objective of 'creating an organisation that can match the best telecommunications company anywhere in the world' had included the following:

1979: The Government announced the reorganisation of the General Post Office through the separation of its telecommunications services from its postal and banking services.
1981: The Act of Parliament setting up the new British Telecommunications corporation received Royal Assent on 27 July and the corporation came into being on 1 October 1981.

1982:   The Government announced plans to turn British Telecommunications Corporation into a public limited company.

1983:   The British Telecom Unions Committee (BTUC) launched a massive campaign against privatisation alleging that the inevitable thrust for profits would dictate adverse BT policies and attitudes towards its customers and personnel. The Post Office Engineers Union (POEU) commenced a programme of industrial action.

1984:   The Telecommunications Act enabled British Telecom to be transformed from a public corporation into a public limited company.

1985:   British Telecom plc came into being. The selling of 51 per cent of shares realised £4bn. 80 per cent of British Telecom staff used their own money to buy shares over and above their allocation of free shares.

1986:   Competition, already active in the customer services market, is also introduced into the more lucrative telephone network market. The Government granted a licence to Mercury Communications Ltd which is owned jointly by Cable & Wireless (40 per cent), British Petroleum (40 per cent) and Barclays Merchant Bank (20 per cent).

Management could also look back, in 1987, using a functional perspective, to view British Telecom's more recent, privatised, developments.

Financial performance since privatisation, for example, in terms of turnover and profits had been improving by more than 10 per cent each year. A variety of performance and other statistics is available in Appendix 13.1 and is worth perusal at this stage.

Financial strength had enabled BT to become a huge investor in *R&D* activities. R&D expenditure, planned at £2,100m (up 35 per cent on 1984 levels) evidenced the longer term aspirations and plans of the BT management. The massive investment programme in this area since privatisation was a stimulator of some of the 1987 developments being undertaken by BT:

The network: Inland telephone call volume was growing at a rate of around 7 per cent per annum, overseas calls at a rate of 13 per cent per annum. In 1985, 'cellnet', BT's joint venture with Securicor had been launched. Modern digital systems were now being installed at the rate of one every working day. Recently, work had begun on a £50m optical fibre network linking BT's customers in the City of London.

New systems   As part of a £700m computerisation programme, the directory
and service: enquiry and customer service systems were being updated and improved.

The community: A £160m programme to modernise payphones had already provided a higher total number of payphones than had existed two years earlier, with over half having modern equipment and many taking Phonecards.

Satellite   BT had always been a world leader in satellite commun-
communication: ications. Earth stations in Cornwall and Hertfordshire together link the UK with more than 100 countries. A third earth

station, the London Teleport, transmits six TV channels around the UK and Europe.

Sir George Jefferson told shareholders that BT's continuing strength made it possible to invest more than ever before to improve the service to customers and secure the future prosperity of the company for shareholders and staff alike.

In a *marketing* sense Telecom was now clearly perceived as a commercially orientated service. It was the UK's second largest advertiser with a promotional budget of over £40m.

'Busby', 'It's for You-Hoo' and the 'Animals' media campaigns had helped to stimulate growing numbers of telephone calls (a central objective of BT during recent years). 'Live' testing of ads – Telecom literally measured the number of calls made after each showing of the three ads – had been applauded for its ingenuity. However, the fact that figures were never divulged led to rumours that the 'It's for You-Hoo' campaign had been dropped not for its lack of success but more because Telecom did not get on with its account team at the agency 'KMP'. Four agencies presently share the BT account – each with its own target market to appeal to (JWT – 'residential users'; Abbott and Mead 'individual customers at work'; Bartle Bogle – 'individual customers in a management role'; Colmans – 'specialist audiences' (such as the tourist industry)).

While competition was only slowly making its presence felt in the telephone network market, more intense competition in the equipment market maintained lower levels of profitability in this sector. Nevertheless, the equipment market was viewed as a complementary and necessary adjunct to successful business in the more lucrative network segment.

Despite declared objectives of more flexible, efficient and attractive customer interactions and products/services BT had been subjected to growing criticism over standards of customer service. Accusations of a declining standard of service and higher charges – particularly in the context of domestic customers – prevailed.

In 1987, MPs referred, in the House of Commons, to BT's abuse of monopoly power and its appalling treatment of customers. The National Consumer Council produced a 1987 report which alleged a worsening service record. The Telecommunication Users' Association joined the criticism bandwagon claiming a marked deterioration in service – for business and domestic users alike.

Complaints were about crossed lines, high costs, crackling connections, and the length of time being taken to install new systems and/or make repairs to existing ones. The NCC also complained that since privatisation, BT had stopped publishing its quality of service measurements because of their 'commercial sensitivity'. The TUA blamed the poor performance in part, on too few engineers.

The Office of Telecommunications (OFTEL), the Government created consumer-orientated 'watchdog' and regulator also added fuel to the argument against BT's customer service record with its 1987 report which concurred that standards seemed to be falling (48 per cent of people wanting to use a call box had been unable to find one that was working, for example). The director general of OFTEL, Professor Bryan Carsberg, said 'BT has insufficient incentive under the present arrangement to repair faults quickly and to accept a contract commitment for dates for providing a new service.' He threatened the introduction of a system of financial penalties against BT if its record did not improve.

In response to such criticisms, BT management steadfastly refuted them, claiming instead that:

1   Service had, in fact, improved since privatisation (the chairman's 1986 speech to shareholders, for example, had referred to the 1980 list of 250,000 people hoping for the chance of a phone – with virtually no choice of equipment – and compared this to the wide choice now available and the lack of any significant waiting list).
2   Complaints had increased because of publicity surrounding the privatisation of BT.
3   Some problems were inevitable because of:
     (a) years of under investment in a nationalised industry;
     (b) the need to handle an exercise equivalent, according to one BT spokesman, to changing engines on Concorde in mid-Atlantic.

BT management felt that the growing levels of competition were sufficient sources of regulation to ensure acceptable consumer responsiveness.

City analysts tended to agree with Telecom's perceptions in this area feeling, generally, that what was being witnessed were the natural re-birth pangs of an industry converting itself into a commercial organisation and undergoing a technological revolution.

If consumers felt unhappy about their interactions with Telecom, *personnel* seemed even more dissatisfied with its situation since privatisation. Clerical and engineering staff were concerned that job losses (see Appendix 13.2) would become *the* means for increasing profits. New technology seemed set to make inroads into labour intensive areas of work such as exchange maintenance and operator services. The BT organisational objectives of efficiency through the streamlining of workforces, the introduction of more flexible working practices and the implementation of new technology was, in the eyes of many staff, translating into job insecurity and worsening job conditions. Unions accused BT management and the Government of going back on promises of 'no job losses through privatisation'. In a radio debate, Bill Chatham, for BT's management, claimed that job losses had been created only through natural wastage. Brian Kenny for the clerical union countered that increasing workloads justified the *creation* of jobs and that as a major employer, BT had a responsibility to be a provider of jobs and not a destroyer of them.

In conversation, rank and file staff agreed that their levels of pay were comparatively high and felt that the industrial unrest within the organisation was not so much about wages but more about a reaction to a new aggressive and callous management style and a lack of recognition for the contribution they were making to the commercial success of BT. They also felt resentful of the fact that a perceived need to introduce more commercially orientated managements had produced an inequitable move towards increasing the size of management at a time when the workforce was being pressed to produce more for less.

In early 1987, a 76 per cent vote in favour of industrial action by NCU clerical group members was in direct contradiction to management claims that BT's staff had been happy with their pay and conditions since privatisation. Appendix 13.2 offers information on both sides to the dispute. In January 1987, engineers came out on strike after management had reportedly locked them out for refusing to sign pledges of normal working.

The unions' standpoint summarised by John Golding, the NCU's General Secretary, had remained consistent since the news that BT was to be privatised ... 'higher prices, new charges and lower quality of service are faults which will not be cleared until BT's top management stop putting profits first'. Neither did the unions have confidence in OFTEL as an adequate overseer/regulator of the telecommunications industry. Rather the call was for a return to public ownership with Mercury, 'the cream-skimming competition' inside BT.

Three years on from privatisation, then, British Telecom's top management had many favourable results and resources to reflect on during the course of any strategic evaluation which they might have undertaken. Despite environmental problems and growing competition, a number of opportunities for further development and growth would also be apparent from such an exercise. Plainly evident, also, however, were a number of 'crossed wires' which clearly and urgently demanded application of top management's planning and decision-making skills.

Three years on, again, in 1990, and the BT management was in the middle of a quality and productivity based organisation culture change programme (see Appendix 13.3). The 1990s seemed set to present a challenging era of change and more change. Appendices 13.4 and 13.5 provide information on the range and nature of BT's activities in the early 1990s and some of the financial and other performances achieved.

Appendix 13.1(a) *Financial performance of British Telecom*

Financial year ending 31 Mar.	1973	1975	1977	1979	1980	1981	1982	1983	1984	1985	1986	1987	1988[1]
Turnover (£m)	1,002	1,388	2,658	3,258	3,601	4,570	5,763	6,414	6,876	7,653	8,387	9,424	7,556
Pre-tax profit (£m)	N/A	N/A	N/A	N/A	317	570	936	1,031	990	1,480	1,810	2,067	1,694
Return on capital employed	N/A	N/A	N/A	N/A	N/A	N/A	N/A	19.3%	17.5%	19.1%	20.9%	21.9%	N/A
Total number of employees	N/A	N/A	N/A	N/A	N/A	N/A	253,262	245,976	241,174	238,304	233,711	236,461	N/A

Notes: [1] 9 months to December only
▼ time of privatisation

Source: Observer (DataStream)

124 Public sector organisations

Appendix 13.1(b) *Share performance of British Telecom*

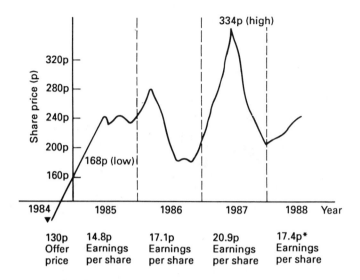

Notes: * 9 months to December only
▼ Time of privatisation

Source: *Sunday Telegraph*

Appendix 13.1(c) *British Telecom recorded complaints*

Year	Complaints
1985	10,000
1986	16,000
1987	24,000

Appendix 13.1(d) *British Telecom Price changes*

		Nov. 1981	May 1982	Nov. 1983	Nov. 1984	Nov. 1985	Nov. 1986	Nov. 1987
Rental Line & phone		+12.5%	N/A	+4.8%	+7.1%	+8.5%	+3.7%	0%
Local calls	Peak	+7.5%	N/A	+2.3%	+6.8%	+6.4%	+18.9%	0%
	Standard	+115%	N/A	+2.3%	+6.8%	+6.4%	+6.4%	0%
	Cheap	+7.5%	N/A	+2.5%	+6.8%	+6.4%	–3.6%	0%
Trunk calls	Peak	+7.5%	–33%	+2.3%	–11%	–15%	–12%	0%
	Standard	+34%	–40%	+2.6%	–5%	–20%	–12%	0%
	Cheap	+20%	–24.9%	+2.3%	+6.4%	+6%	–12%	0%

Source: OFTEL (1987)

Appendix 13.1(e) *Charge comparison*

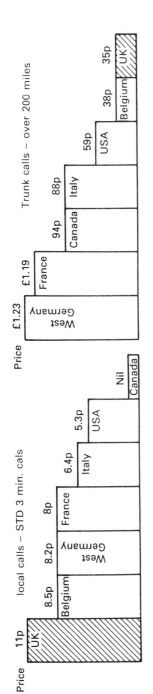

local calls – STD 3 min. cals

	UK	Belgium	West Germany	France	Italy	USA	Canada
Price	11p	8.5p	8.2p	8p	6.4p	5.3p	Nil

Trunk calls – over 200 miles

	West Germany	France	Canada	Italy	USA	Belgium	UK
Price	£1.23	£1.19	94p	88p	59p	38p	35p

Overseas calls – between capitals

	Belgium	Italy	West Germany	France	Canada	USA	UK
Price	£6.15	£5.85	£3.93	£3.15	£2.86	£2.42	£1.85

Telephone system	Customer lines per employee
Holland	200
Canada (Bell)	185
Italy	158
Japan (NTT)	151
New York (NYNEX)	151
France	138
Spain	129
Germany	122
Sweden	110
UK (BT)	94

Source: The Financial Times (April 1987)

Appendix 13.2

WE'VE HAD ENOUGH!

- Pay offer rejected!
- Massive vote for industrial action!
- Members walkout in protest!

NCU clerical group members in British Telecom voted to take industrial action and rejected BT's insulting pay offer, thereby bursting the bubble of Ian Vallance's day dream assertions that BT's staff are happy with their pay and conditions of service since privatisation.

Following the ballot which resulted in 76% members voting to reject the offer, members walked out in disgust at the end of their core time, on Monday, 24th November.

Management's immediate response was to threaten suspensions and loss of pay and even the ending of flexitime until the end of the dispute.

Such was the resolve of the membership, that in the face of this provocation many members were reluctant to go back the following day.

Indeed members have been so angered by BT's intent to dock pay for the hours they were absent that many branches are taking legal advice and challenging BT's right to deduct pay for hours they were not contracted to work.

Management's tactics have been to try and instil fear in our members whilst at the same time they have attempted to persuade them that the pay offer is generous.

British Telecom are devoted to a propaganda war of truth bending.

Despite this our members are aware of the justice of their case in pursuing a wage increase that recognises the part they have played in BT's success and that does not contain strings which will worsen their conditions of service and job prospects.

The message is clear! We are sick of increasing workloads! We are sick of the use of overtime to reduce staffing levels! We are sick of the manipulation of flexitime by management. We are sick of no reward for the massive amount of profits we make each year! We want recognition by management of the successes we have made for British Telecom.

ENGINEERS PLEDGE SUPPORT

Dave Morris, Chairperson of the Engineering Groups Pay Committee pledged the Engineering group's support for a joint pay campaign and joint industrial action with the Clerical Group. Speaking at the Broad Strategy conference, he said, "We are not going to leave the common table bargaining that we are in. We'll be with you in two weeks time. The engineering group will be strongly supporting your executive and we are strongly committed to a common settlement!"

Appendix 13.3(a) *Experts in communication*

Mike Bett, vice-chairman of BT and a companion of the BIM is confident of the benefits of his organisation's cultural changes.

British Telecom has been much in the press this year – with attention centred on two major strands of change. One of these comes from outside the company – the duopoly review which will shape the future of telecommunications in the UK during the 1990s. The other is generated by the company's management board and is a far-reaching reorientation and restructuring of the company, to put customers first and to make sure of continued success in demanding global market places. This initiative is known as Project Sovereign.

This heralds a new way of focusing on customers – a new culture. These are big ambitions, magnified further by the scale of the organisation itself. With over 25 million customers in Britain alone, the 230,000 British Telecom people are based at around 8,000 locations in the UK and there is a rapidly growing number around the world.

Although BT is often seen as a technology-driven company, its future achievements will concern people – its people and its customers. To continue to be successful and maintain competitive advantage, quality and satisfaction must be built into every customer relationship.

BT has invested wisely in strategic analysis, and it was close attention to strategic imperatives that convinced the BT board that 1990 was the year for change. It took this decision aware that it would be difficult for many of its people to understand why such change was necessary when things were going well. During the 1980s many UK companies were galvanised into change by worsening market performance but BT decided to change from a position of strength. It was able to use the time to make major changes in a thorough way, rather than using a sense of crisis to jolt its managers.

In the packages of change launched by chairman, Iain Vallance on 29 March, a new framework for the company's organisation is a key strand. For many years, BT has been structured in a way which reflects the historic dominance in the business of telephone service to UK customers. This has supported a very large UK division (with around 200,000 people) which has found it difficult to focus on specific customer needs.

From April 1991 this will be restructured into a total of seven major units providing a basis for building flatter organisations within each division. The move towards less layers is central to BT's restructuring. Historically, British Telecom has made much use of 'general management' and has in recent years had as many as five layers of general management sitting above functionally orientated managers. This brought benefits during the transition of BT into the private sector, encouraging an entrepreneurial style, but now the drive is for more targeted management and teamwork across the functions.

The Project Sovereign guidelines about management layers are clear – a maximum of six layers between the chairman and those below management level. This is not a universal paradigm; in many cases fewer layers are found to be necessary, and in a handful of cases a seventh is added. The process of building the new divisions during the 1990 financial year has given BT time to review critically every aspect of the planned structures and to identify unnecessary and overlapping roles. Already BT is seeing the benefits of fewer layers; fewer blockages in communication, more honesty, more debate, and more responsiveness when action is urgent.

Project Sovereign also helps BT to understand the different needs of its senior professional staff. Historically, managerial and professional people have been part of a common pay and grading structure. Now, through different norms for everyone in its struture design, and through a company-wide programme of job assessment, it will be able to recognise the different contributions which each group makes.

BT's use of clear, simple structural rules has allowed no ambiguity about Iain Vallance's intent, but has not removed the pain from the change process. Many of its people were very comfortable in their former posts and found it a personal and professional challenge to face up to the changes. Some – around 5,000 in total – will have left the company by March 1991 through an early release scheme. For others, major change has brought new opportunities and career development. So much change in such a short time puts a premium on good, honest communication. Understandably, the prime concern for each individual is 'what will it mean for me?' and it has been difficult to express the full import of the changes quickly enough and personally enough to satisfy its managers. BT has sought to balance speed with equity of treatment across its very large managerial workforce. I now think it has struck a fair balance.

What it will have created by April 1991, throughout the company, is a platform fit for the decade ahead; an underpinning organisation which will bring benefit to its customers and provide sharpened, more rewarding jobs for its managers. Of course, it expects to be held accountable for what it's doing in the most public way of all – by the customers it answers to.

Appendix 13.3(b) *A leaner, fitter BT*

Chairman Iain Vallance – 'The customer must come first. We need to understand our customers' requirements and meet them efficiently.'

The next phase of changes in the way British Telecom is structured – designed to make the company more able to meet the needs of particular types of customers – has been unveiled by chairman Iain Vallance. He has also announced the first wave of senior appointments.

In the powerful, up-beat message to staff Mr Vallance said: 'We are going to drive up our revenues by understanding our customer's needs in depth and by meeting them more effectively and efficiently than our competitors anywhere in the world. It is positive, not defensive, it is outgoing, not introverted. And, best of all, it is fun, not just a grind.'

Project Sovereign, the initiative launched on 29 March aimed at Putting Customers First, does not represent change for change sake. It makes a funamental shift in the company's culture to being more customer-friendly. Mr Vallance said: 'One theme is all-important. The customer must come first. We need to understand our customer's requirements and meet them efficiently. To do this, we must be able to focus on the differing needs of our many markets, and to respond quickly to those needs, with a leaner, fitter organisation designed to encourage fast decision-taking and improved communications.'

A streamlining of the organisation will involve a reduction of between 4,000 and 5,000 in the numbers of managers in the company by April next year. Mr Vallance explained, 'We will be operating an early release scheme for managers that I believe will be attractive for those who do not have a place in the new organisation.... We are determined that everyone will receive fair and sympathetic treatment, in line with the values of our company.'

Details of the early release scheme will be announced in due course.

The new BT – with its customer-facing divisions, Personal Communications and Business Communications – will grow out of the old by 1 April 1991. Supporting both the new divisions will be Worldwide Networks, which will combine the company's UK and international networks in one. A Special Business Division will handle activities which are best managed separately; Products and Services Management will manage the products and services portfolio for the customer-facing divisions; and Developments and Procurement will provide a broad spectrum of technical services.

Mr Vallance has announced the names of those who will lead three new divisions.

* Mike Armitage will become managing director, Personal Communications.
* David Dey will be managing director, Business Communications. Nick Kane will be deputy managing director, and will be reponsible for marketing and business planning.
* Anthony Booth will be managing director, Worldwide Networks.

Mr Vallance said that, although the new field structures cover larger areas than the current UK districts, they will not lead to greater centralisation. He explained, 'We still have our teams of people on the ground, serving their local communities.... Over the next few weeks we will also be finalising our arrangements for representation of BT in local communities, recognising the special needs of Scotland and Wales, where we expect to appoint resident senior managers supported by National Advisory Forums.'

Mr Vallance added, 'The new organisation is not an end in itself. It provides the framework for a complete culture change in BT.... It will be a culture where we sell, instead of take orders; where we find ways of doing what the customer wants, instead of reasons for not doing it; where we rely on teamwork, instead of office politics; where we can carry through to the next stage that marathon of total quality management, and finally get quality into the bloodstream.'

Appendix 13.3(c) *Telecom Sovereign November 1990 – questions and answers*

Q How will Sovereign affect the long-term future of ETGs, clerical staff, operators, and other ancillary staff? Will their jobs be secure?

A Sovereign is all about creating an organisation and culture that makes it easy and natural to devote energies to serving customers in a quality way. While no long-term guarantees can be given about any job in any organisation a successful company will need good people for customer-facing roles and support roles.

Q Will staff who are not managers be subject to the same style of job cuts and/or early release schemes as managers?

A Changes in structure which are part of Sovereign primarily affect management posts within BT. It is anticipated that most non-managers will transfer into the new organisation with their current work. There are, therefore, no current plans for job cuts and/or early release schemes, beyond existing announcements about individual work areas such as catering.

Q What happened to the regular information about Sovereign which we were promised? Apart from Telecom Today and the district newspapers, we get very little passed to us by our managers?

Why are we told information will be passed to us only when our managers consider it necessary? Don't they trust us to be able to understand the aims of Sovereign without their vetting of the documented information available

A   There is no intention to restrict information about Sovereign within BT. Any item contained in *Management News* (or its insert, *Sovereign Update*), can be circulated by whatever channels were in place for this purpose prior to Sovereign. We have increased coverage in *Telecom Today* to ensure that everyone does receive up-to-date information about Sovereign. Briefs for team meetings are also being circulated to ensure that managers are well-equipped to brief their people.

Q   Will the new structure of the company mean that some staff will find that their job has changed beyond recognition?

A   Again, most changes to the shape of jobs will be to management jobs. Others will generally be doing a similar job as they are now. Some jobs may be more focused than at present, for example on business or personal customers rather than a mix.

Q   Why is Project Sovereign taking so long to happen?

A   We are aware that the length of implementation of Sovereign is causing uncertainty for many of our people. However, the alternative would have been to rush into a massive change totally unprepared. We are aiming to implement Sovereign in a quality way and this does take a huge amount of planning. Some of the biggest tasks are defining each part of the organisation in detail then checking the organisation plans to ensure that no duplication exists and that every area of work is accounted for. Following on from this is the allocation of people to jobs, and in parallel are all the budgetary and systems changes needed to support the new organisation.

Q   Is the programme on schedule?

A   Yes, Sovereign is on schedule. Some parts of the Sovereign organisations are already in place (Sales, Private Services London, Operator Services). The new organisation will be fully in place by 2 April 1991.

Q   Will there be any promotion into the Managerial and Professional Group (MPG) in the coming months?

A   If there are no suitable substantive MPG candidates for managerial and professional jobs in the new organisation, then there may be the opportunity for promotion, in line with the existing arrangements.

Q   What happens to people on temporary promotion to management grades?

A   The Sovereign appointments process initially just considers substantive managers. Individual cases will be clarified once the final numbers of people needed for each work function in the new organisation are known.

Q   What about TQM – is it still alive?

A   Yes, very much so! Sovereign can be viewed as the next phase of TQM, in terms of 'doing what we do better'. The culture change aspect of Sovereign is all bout getting TQM into the bloodstream of BT. An important part of this will be the launch of 'Involving Everyone' in April 1991.

Q Whose idea was Project Sovereign?

A The initial Sovereign proposals came from a TQM project called SCOOP – which pulled together all the recent work on how BT can better organise to meet customer needs more effectively – in view of the need for BT to be even better at serving its customers in the face of increasing competition and increasing global opportunity. Since Sovereign implementation has begun, many managers in all parts of the organisation have been working on the detail via hundreds of Sovereign projects. In this way, all BT managers 'own' Sovereign, although it is very much spearheaded by the chairman and his Management Board.

Q Will re-location out of London continue under Sovereign?

A It is anticipated that at 1 April 1991 most managers will continue to work at or near where they are now. As the new organisation settles down there is likely to be some rationalisation. Relocation out of London will remain an aim, where possible, and will support the Sovereign objective of eliminating unnecessary cost.

Q How will the new BT divisions fit together when the company is restructured next April?

A The organisational chart published here answers your question. The customer, who comes at the bottom of the old structure, will be at the top – with everyone in BT in business to support him or her.

Business Communications, Personal Communications and Special Businesses are in place to serve the customer, supported by all other parts of the company.

Project Sovereign

Putting customers first –
British Telecom
organisation
at 2 April 1991

Customers and markets		
Business communications	Personal communications	Special businesses

Products and services management

Worldwide networks

Development and procurement

Group HQ (strategy, finance, personnel, etc.)

Appendix 13.3(d) *British Telecom* Management News – *November/December 1990*

TQM REMAINS THE KEY TO BT'S SUCCESS

The going may be getting tough in the demanding programme to reshape British Telecom, but chairman Iain Vallance has signalled that now is the time for additional determination and commitment.

And with this in mind, he has set senior managers a series of stretching targets and objectives for the next five years and called for a return to the basics of Total Quality Management.

Last month Mr Vallance told senior managers at the Chairman's Conference in Bournemouth: 'This year we have launched the most fundamental Quality project we have ever undertaken – in the form of Project Sovereign – with the explicit objective of shaping up to putting our customers first.

'And let's face it – it's hard going.'

He reminded the conference that TQM is a marathon and not a sprint and added, 'When the going is at its most painful – which to be honest, it is just now – then is the time to bring out that additional determination and commitment to improvement.'

The inevitable undercurrent of uncertainty generated by Sovereign needed to be handled professionally and positively.

And to guide his management team back to the TQM basics with this in mind, Mr Vallance distilled British Telecom's values into five 'one-liners':

- We put our customers first
- We are professional
- We respect each other
- We work as one team
- We are committed to continuous improvement

The chairman stressed that the leadership of the company should reflect the five values in its everyday business and that managers should lay themselves open to criticism from all BT people 'to help us to improve'.

In the drive to pump Quality round the BT bloodstream, Mr Vallance unveiled blueprints by which TQM would be built into every operation in BT.

He outlined quality 'imperatives', aimed at building on BT's strengths, and remedying its weaknesses.

The first is: **We must drive quality from the top**.

To address this need, Mr Vallance told the conference that every major unit in the new BT must have a Quality Council attended by all senior managers. He added that every senior manager will:

- Attend, and subsequently lead, the Leadership Programme events
- Maintain continuous contact with customers
- Have face-to-face contact with all their people at least once a year
- Include Quality targets in their Quality Plan and Budgets

The second of the chairman's Quality imperatives is: **We must pursue excellence in customer service**.

And to provide a single goal for that excellence, he called for a 90 per cent reduction in customer service failures throughout the company by 1995.

Performance
The chairman's challenge to senior managers would mean an installation and fault clearance performance, as well as a payphone serviceability level, of up to 99 per cent.

'To achieve a step-change improvement of that order implies a commensurate reduction in failure costs over the five-year period', he said.

The five-year plan for each division and function must be geared to that goal, starting from 1991/2.

Appendix 13.3(e) *Aspects of BT: productivity improvement system*

Measuring operational effectiveness

Three streams of information

- Cost measure
- Manhour measure
- Quality measure

Tiered structure

- Tier 1 – 16 ratios
- Tier 2 – 25 ratios
- Tier 3 – class of work/account code ratios

Tier 1 ratios

1	Provision of exchange lines (including Telex)
2	Provision of private circuits
3	Provision of CPE products
4	Use of restoration of exchange lines
4.1	Local lines maintenance
4.2	Local exchange maintenance
4.3	Main exchange maintenance
4.4	Trunk and junction transmission maintenance
4.5	Repair controls
5	Private circuit direct maintenance
6	CPE maintenance
7.1	Operator service (DA)

7.2   Operator services (OA)
8   Public payphone maintenance and support
9.1   Billing excluding bad debts and provision change
9.2   Billing bad debts and provision change

Tier 2 ratio activities

10.1 Depreciation: local line
10.2 Depreciation: local exchange
10.3 Depreciation: junction transmission
10.4 Depreciation: other
11   Planning and development
12.1 Supplies
12.2 Transport
13   Marketing and sales
14   Computing
15   Accommodation
16.1 Pers and admin excl. TRG
16.2 Pers and admin TRG only
17   General management and misc.
18   Common P&I services and others
19   Network repayment works maintenance
20   Rates on installation
21   Network non-FAR maintenance
22   Common T&S
23   Common other maintenance and intercorp.
24   Accounting and management services
25   Phonebooks
26   Operator management
27   Total expenditure transfers (excl. intercorp.)
28   Total other operating income
29   Total operating costs

Provision and installation – exchange connections inc. Telex (Tier 1)

Manhour ratio
Engineering manhours per exchange and telex lines supplied

Cost ratio
Cost £s per exchange and Telex lines supplied

Quality measures
Business appointment orders completed in next six working days or CLD
Business programmed orders completed in six weeks or CLD
Residential appointment orders completed in next eight working days or CLD

Telex orders completed by target – (ten working days) or CLD
Telephone orders completed by CCD

Public payphone maintenance and support (Tier 1)

Manhour ratio
Manhour per mean public payphone

Cost ratio
Cost £s per mean public payphone

Quality measures
Public payphones serviceability

Use by districts

1   Setting of targets
2   Monitoring of achievement against targets/budgets by DGM and District
    Board members. Build into Bonus Schemes.
    NB Monitoring of achievement by L1, L2 and L3 managers will be done
    with the District MCS (Management Control System)
3   Comparison of results within group of similar districts – and wider if
    desired.
4   Preparation of AOP data in conjunction with HQ guidance.

Appendix 13.3(f) *It's our best yet!*

The Company's investment of £8m a day to provide the country with
world-class telecommunications is paying off. The quality of service given to
customers has reached an all-time high on nearly every front.

   BT's quality of service report for the six months to September shows that:

*   Of the 80 million calls made every day, 99 out of 100 get through at the
    first attempt
*   Nearly 88 per cent of calls to Directory Enquiries get through at the first
    attempt and seven out of eight of those are answered within 15 seconds
*   Ninety-six per cent of BT's 95,000 public payphones are in full working
    order at any one time
*   And, on average, a fault on a line will occur only once every six years

Mike Bett, vice-chairman said 'The investment is paying off. It is helping us to
drive down fault rates, speed up our repair service, and generally meet our
customers' needs more effectively.

   'Nearly 11 million customers are now connected to local digital exchanges.
And more than 70 per cent of customers are served by modern digital or

electronic exchanges offering faster connections, clearer lines and fewer call failures.'

On average, more than two digital local exchanges are brought into service every working day.

During the six-month period the UK became the first major country to have an entirely digital long-distance telecommunications network as BT completed the modernisation of its trunk network.

The speed of repair service increased substantially during the period (see panel).

Repair Service

	Sept. 89	March 90	Sept. 90
% business faults clear in five working hours	75.9	79.2	88.7
% residential faults cleared in nine working hours	79.4	66.8	87.6
% faults cleared in one working day	86.3	77.5	91.4

Provision of service has been faster, too. The percentage of business orders completed in six working days rose from 67.9 per cent in March to 76.7 per cent in September.

Appendix 13.4 *BT working for the customer*

Customers continue to benefit as emphasis shifts to providing even greater value for money while maintaining hard-won quality of service in a difficult economic situation and against growing competition.

We had a successful year in serving our 25 million customers in the UK, in spite of the difficult economic climate and growing competition. The volume of inland calls rose by 10 per cent while the number of connections increased by 10 per cent (business) and 2.9 per cent (residential). The percentage of public payphones in working order was maintained at 95 per cent and the total in use increased by 4,000 to more than 90,000. There was faster provision of service.

Speed of repair was affected by the succession of winter storms. An emergency plan, drawn up after the 1987 hurricane, was put into operation by British Telecom when the storms of January and February struck. An emergency control centre in London co-ordinated repair operations, switching men and materials around the country and keeping inconvenience to customers to the minimum.

World-class service

British Telecom's worldwide goals are based on providing a world-class service for our UK customers – and concern for customers influences everything we do. In the UK we are making a massive capital investment, running at the rate of more than £12m every working day, to modernise, extend and improve our network and services.

The long-distance network is now fully digital. More than 65 per cent of customers are served by modern exchanges; two digital exchanges are brought into service every day, and millions more customers now have clearer lines, faster connections and specialised services such as itemised billing, already available to more than one-third of our customers.

Last year we laid a further 354,000 kilometres of optical cable and the total now in the network of almost one million kilometres is a higher proportion of fibre than in any other major telecommunications company.

Modernisation is going ahead especially fast in Edinburgh, which has been dubbed the 'Telezone' and singled out to become a live test-bed for British Telecom's most modern technology with service five years ahead of the rest of the country.

Operator services
Further modernisation was carried out to the directory enquiry service, now handling some 800 million calls a year (up 21 per cent). Acute congestion in London has been overcome by opening eight centres around the UK.

Many customers of the directory enquiry service are benefiting from a new computerised voice reproduction system that allows each operator to handle up to 20 per cent more calls.

Operator services in general are now undergoing a fundamental change which will see a screen-based system replacing older-style switchboards. As with the new direct enquiry methods, staff have greeted the new system enthusiastically. Customers are noticing the difference in speed and efficiency.

London code changes
Another problem affecting London was the shortage of telephone numbers as the demand for service has intensified. The solution, which effectively doubles the numbers available for customers, was to replace the familiar 01 prefix with 071 (inner London) and 081 (outer London) from 6 May 1990. After 18 months' planning the changeover went without a hitch.

Customer links
There were closer links with customers throughout the country – more than eight million customers (20 per cent up on the previous year) called at our 40 high street shops to pay bills, make enquiries or buy or rent equipment. A campaign directed at residential customers brought 400,000 requests for a catalogue of products and services.

Customers themselves are making an increasingly important input into our thinking through a country-wide network of consumer liaison panels who work with our local managers to tackle such diverse subjects as sales and installation procedures, indebtedness and giving a better service to users of fax machines.

We are committed to creating an environment which enables every employee to contribute to British Telecom's success through teamwork. In turn, our people are able to share in the company's success through employee share schemes.

Last year some 202,000 employees were given a further opportunity to build a stake in the company through the allocation to each of 56 free shares worth £145 and more than 50,000 employees joined a savings scheme linked to an opportunity to buy 66 million shares in five years' time at a fixed price.

The wide range of training activities and initiatives, costing more than £260m, demonstrated the company's commitment in this area. British Telecom is playing a prominent part in setting high standards for future tele-communications workers, through the Telecommunications Vocational Standards Council, and is also involved with a number of training and enterprise councils.

The number of employees in the group rose by 1,200 to 245,700. In the main telecommunications operations numbers fell by 2,000.

Equal opportunities

Initiatives to encourage women in management and non-traditional jobs continue and the successful programme to retrain non-technical women employees as technicians is now in its fourth year.

All job applications are to be ethnically monitored and a follow-up programme covering all staff is being considered.

Welfare, health and safety

British Telecom encourages the recruitment, employment and – through retraining schemes and the provision of special equipment – the retention of people with disabilities. Our Occupational Health Service continues to offer employees health screening services.

As part of our continuing commitment to safety, a campaign to cut the accident rate within the company by half over the next five years has been started. Safety training will be stepped up and the professionalism of safety staff will be improved.

We continue to consult and negotiate with the unions. The programme of regular communications with staff was reinforced by a series of 'Whicker's Telecom World' videos designed to be shown and discussed at team meetings.

Appendix 13.5 Financial and other performance details

Summary financial statement

This summary financial statement has been drawn up under the provisions of the Companies Act. It is a summary of information contained elsewhere in the 1990 Report and Accounts.

Summary directors' report

The underlying strength of British Telecom was reflected in an increase of 11.2 per cent in our turnover in spite of the effects of adverse economic trends and growing competition. There was strong growth in demand for our services, with the total number of connections to our UK network up by 4.5 per cent at 25 million.

Inland telephone call volumes rose by 10 per cent while international calls were up by 13 per cent. Our mobile services showed particularly strong growth and significant investment was undertaken to maintain our competitiveness.

Our major investment was in capital assets, where we spent £3,115m, to improve the quality and range of our services, expand the network and to keep up the pace of our massive modernisation programme.

This investment, together with more efficient working methods, produced significant improvements to key elements of our UK service. There were improvements in the provision of service and the time taken to make repairs, and the availability of public payphones was maintained at a very high level nationally, while the number of payphones in service was increased by 4,000 to a total of more than 90,000.

Our overseas expansion continued, with major acquisitions in the United States and a strengthening of our organisation there and elsewhere to enable us to serve our customers more effectively.

Research, on which we spent £228m, was closely aligned to the commercial requirements of the group. There was heavy emphasis on improvements to mobile services, the use of optical fibres, and sophisticated computer technology.

The use of technology to improve the quality of life for disabled and elderly people was an important aspect of both our research and our work in the community. Our community activities span a wide range, from working to strengthen the ties between education and business to sponsorship of the arts and environmental projects. Last year we contributed more than £12m, in cash and in kind, to community affairs.

At the end of the year fundamental changes in the structure of the group were announced, to be introduced over the next 12 months with a streamlining of management. The objective is to align the group more closely to the requirements of customers.

Summary group profit and loss account for the year ended 31 March 1990

| | 1990
£m | 1989
£m |
|---|---|---|
| *Turnover* | 12,315 | 11,071 |
| Operating costs | 9,105 | 8,264 |
| (including group's share of losses, less | | |
| profits of related companies £6m (1989–£19m)) | | |
| *Operating profit* | 3,210 | 2,807 |
| Employee profit sharing | 34 | 30 |
| Net interest payable | 484 | 340 |

	1990 £m	1989 £m
Profit before exceptional charge and taxation	2,692	2,437
Exceptional charge[1]	390	–
Profit on ordinary activities before taxation	2,302	2,437
Tax on profit on ordinary activities	767	858
Profit on ordinary activities after taxation	1,535	1,579
Minority interests	26	13
Preference dividends	–	2
Profit attributable to ordinary shareholders	1,509	1,564
Ordinary dividends	720	634
Retained profit for the financial year	789	930
Earnings per ordinary share	25.0p	25.9p
Earnings per ordinary share before exceptional charge	29.2p	25.9p
Dividends per ordinary share	11.8p	10.5p

Notes:[1] A provision of £390m was made in the year ended 31 March 1990 to cover the costs of restructuring the group and refocusing its operations.

Directors' emoluments: The total emoluments of the directors of the company for the year ended 31 March 1990 were £2,106,259 (1989 = £1,757,647).

Summary group balance sheet at 31 March 1990

	1990 £m	1989 £m
Assets employed		
Fixed assets	15,503	13,568
Current assets	3,644	3,770
Creditors: amounts falling due within one year	4,896	4,481
Net current liabilities	(1,252)	(711)
Financed by		
Creditors: amounts falling due after more than one year	4,320	3,622
Provisions for liabilities and charges	595	286
Minority interests	112	100
Capital and reserves	9,224	8,849
	14,251	12,857

The summary financial statement on pages 7 and 9 was approved by the board of directors on 30 May 1990 and was signed on its behalf by
I D T Vallance chairman
B D Romerill group finance Director

Statement by the auditors
to the shareholders of British Telecommunications plc

In our opinion the summary financial statement set out on pages 7 to 9 is consistent with the group's annual financial statement and directors' report and complies with the requirements of section 251 of the Companies Act 1985 and the regulations made thereunder.

Coopers and Lybrand Deloitte
Chartered Accountants
London, 30 May 1990

Financial review
Investment for the future reaches a record £3.1 billion. British Telecom's profit before tax and an exceptional charge was £2,692m, an increase of 10.5 per cent over the previous year. Earnings per share before the exceptional charge were 29.2p, an increase of 12.4 per cent.

Profit before tax for the year after the exceptional charge of £390m was £2,302m. Earnings per share after the exceptional charge were 25p. (The exceptional charge represents the estimated costs of a strategic restructuring of the group, including those of an early release scheme for managers.)

£34m was allocated to employee profit sharing. Taxation accounted for £767m.

The total dividends for the year of 11.8p per share (4.65p interim and 7.15p final) are up by 12.4 per cent on the previous year.

Demand up
Demand for the group's services grew during the year in spite of the slowdown in the UK economy and turnover of £12,315m was 11.2 per cent higher than in the previous year. The main gains were 10 per cent growth in the volume of inland calls and 13 per cent growth in international calls.

Prices for our main United Kingdom telephone services were increased by an average of 3.5 per cent in September 1989 after a price freeze lasting nearly three years.

Operating costs increased by 10.2 per cent to £9,105m.

The healthy financial position of our main pension schemes allowed us to reduce the cost of providing pensions to our staff – while maintaining the security of future pensions. Operating costs benefited by £146m, through this reduction.

Operating profit
Operating profit was 14.4 per cent higher at £3,210m. The interest charge for

the year was £484m (42.4 per cent higher) due to the additional borrowings we made to finance our modernisation programme and investments in North America.

Profit after tax was £1,789m before the exceptional charge, an increase of 13.3 per cent, and £1,535m after the exceptional charge – £254m net of tax.

Investment

Expenditure on new plant, equipment and buildings increased from £2,947m to a record £3,115m, a 5.7 per cent increase. We continued to make considerable progress in changing our telephone exchanges to the modern digital technology and improving the quality of calls with optical fibre cables. Our US investment in McCaw Cellular Communications of £907m during the year and our acquisition of the international Tymet data network business for £231m demonstrated our commitment to global communications.

Although borrowings increased substantially during the year, the balance sheet remains satisfactory.

On the international scene, British Telecom enjoyed another year of record business, connecting Britain to the world and meeting the exploding demand for worldwide telecommunications facilities. Our expanding cable and satellite network is carrying an ever-increasing amount of telephone calls, facsimile messages, computer information and televised material.

The volume of international calls rose by 13 per cent.

The international market

British Telecom's UK customers can now dial their own telephone calls to nearly 200 overseas countries. Helping to spread the habit won a best actress award for Maureen Lipman playing both 'Beattie' and her Australian sister, Rose, in the TV commercials. Business travellers and tourists made 25 per cent more use of our services such as UK Direct to phone from abroad and be billed at home. Demand accelerated for international data network services and we bought a major US business, Tymet. BT Tymet operates internationally and in the USA alone there are some 11,000 simultaneous users of Tymet's public data network, verifying credit cards, making flight reservations or performing other crucial works.

International network

Our third big international digital 'gateway' exchange – gateways link different networks – was opened in London as the proportion of international calls carried through the digital gateways rose to 72 per cent. The first intercontinental high speed switched services were launched to the USA and Japan, marking a further significant step towards true international ISDN services. Optical fibre technology is playing an increasingly important role in international telecommunications; there are now optical fibre links to Japan as well as to many countries in Europe and North America. BT (Marine) has commissioned a new cableship to deal with rising demand.

Customer assistance

Three more international call-connect centres were opened at Grimsby, Leicester and Mansfield. Together with the opening of the new international directory enquiries centre at Grimsby they helped improve the speed of response to customers to a new record. A customer service centre was opened at Burnham, Somerset, to give UK customers a single point of contact for general information on British Telecom's international services.

We aim to become the leading international supplier of communications systems and services. In support of this aim we focused on three fundamental activities:

- Our major investments improved the quality of service on offer
- We continued to strengthen our product portfolio through rationalisation and exclusive distribution arrangements with leading manufacturers
- Our overseas operations were expanded and reorganised to suit customer requirements

Mobile growth

There was rapid growth in the established mobile services – cellular radio telephones and voice messaging. Cellnet, the subsidiary partly owned by Securicor, achieved accelerating growth of its customer base, now approaching the half-million mark, and dramatically increased capacity on the network to improve service quality.

These services are already essential business tools and we are now promoting them to domestic users.

The travelling public will also benefit from the new Phonepoint personal communications (telepoint) service, launched last September, in which British Telecom has a minority shareholding.

Expansion at home was mirrored in the United States, where we completed our acquisition of a 20 per cent stake in the country's leading cellular telephone operator, McCaw Cellular Communications.

Systems solutions

British Telecom also builds advanced communications systems to meet customers' needs for fast transfer and effective display of business information.

These projects range from the worldwide data network we are building for ICI to the more familiar LINK network connecting high street cash dispensers. One of the most important projects underway in this field is a system for administering Britain's imports and exports which we are building for HM Customs.

British Telecom, which is a major supplier of screen-based trading systems, has achieved a significant success in installing nearly 100 financial dealing systems in Europe.

Organisation overseas

In Europe we have offices in eight countries, with some 200 staff serving both

UK-based customers with business on the Continent and European customers with requirements for global communications.

In North America our ability to serve international business customers has been further strengthened by bringing our US-based sales and service operations into a single organisation – British Telecom Inc. – with offices in New York, Chicago, Houston, San Francisco and Los Angeles.

Other activities overseas continued to expand and include winning contracts to supply Singapore with a customer services system and the provision of a network management system to Telefonica, the Spanish telecommunications service.

Our £228m research programme is geared to commercial needs at home and overseas. Latest advances in mobile communications make things easier for the customer on the move.

Commercial basis of research

Behind British Telecom's technological and commercial success lies a £228m annual programme of research and development, closely geared to the needs of our trading divisions and new acquisitions. Activities at our central research and technology laboratories at Martlesham Heath in Suffolk, and our software engineering centres in Ipswich, Belfast, London and Glasgow accounted for £155m. The Queen's Award for Technological Achievement was won by our main optical networks division for the development of opto-electronic receivers used in the first transatlantic undersea optical fibre cable system. We maintained our world lead in the use of optical fibres to improve quality and reduce costs by increasing the distance over which calls can be made without being boosted and increasing the number of simultaneous calls that can be sent down a single fibre.

A trial of the latest fibre systems, involving 400 customers at Bishop's Stortford, Hertfordshire, is supporting our response to the demands of both business and residential customers for new and flexible services.

Sophisticated computer technology is the key to the efficient management of British Telecom's complex digital networks and to many of the new network services which British Telecom offers. Our flexibility in producing innovative services was demonstrated during the nine-month Whitbread Round the World Yacht Race. An award-winning system was devised that indicated competitors' positions throughout the race, disseminated news stories and enabled photographs to be transmitted to land from yachts and mid-ocean.

In mobile communications, trials have been under way to reduce city-centre congestion experienced by cellular telephone users by splitting larger areas into street-sized 'microcells' served by lamppost-mounted transmitters and receivers. And much work has gone into developing advanced messaging systems that will enable users to be 'bleeped' and receive messages on pocket radiopagers across Europe.

Collaboration with our Continental counterparts is aimed at making it possible to use the same cordless telephone at home, in the office and – using public telepoint services – in many European countries.

An important part of our research and development work is to improve service to disabled customers. The latest device to have a successful trial is a videophone which uses cartoon-like images to enable deaf people to hold a sign-language conversation.

British Telecom is committed to making a fitting contribution to the community in which we operate and in the past year we contributed more the £12m, in cash and in kind, to community affairs.

More than 70 British Telecom mangers and staff were seconded to community organisations, to work with job creation agencies and to strengthen the partnerships between industry and education, providing practical help for the health of the community.

Community action

Under the community action programme, we have worked alongside the CBI, Business in the Community and other bodies, to create enterprise opportunities, jobs and training in bringing new life to both towns and country areas.

Progress has continued on inner-city initiatives and on landscaping and reclamation projects aimed at improving local environments.

Charities

In contributing £2.98m to charity we gave special attention to projects which employed new technology to improve the quality of life for elderly people.

Staff contributions to charity in the Give as You Earn scheme have reached more than £315,000. That figure was matched by the company.

Education

Our partnership with education continued to develop. We worked with the Secondary Heads' Association to establish the first assessment centre for head teachers. We expanded our programmes of communications technology workshops and secondments for teachers. We produced new curriculum material for schools, funded language teaching and provided several thousand work experience places. Our chairman, Iain Vallance, is chairman of the Foundation for Education Business Partnerships.

Action for disabled customers

An improved model of the Tribune phone, with better amplification for the hard-of-hearing, was introduced. Other products are being developed to form a new and improved range.

A new edition of the *Guide to Equipment and Services for Disabled Customers* is available, free, from our shops and sales offices.

Sponsorship

There is now a year-round programme of sponsorship, strongly focused on support for national arts tours, environmental projects and schemes involving disabled people.

Our district offices are supporting events around the country – such as the

Lake District Summer Music Festival, the Hallé Orchestra family concerts, Glasgow 1990 – Cultural Capital of Europe, the Royal National Eisteddfod and local environmental projects.

14 · Introducing new technology in the Passport Office

Peter Prowse

Introduction

The Passport Office was part of the Home Office until it became one of the departments planned to be an executive agency in 1991. The Raynor scrutiny of the Passport Office in September 1982 concluded that a computerised passport issuing system would bring great benefits in speeding processing time and increasing productivity. The scrutiny recommended a detailed pilot study to be carried out with the aim of introducing an integrated system as soon as possible after January 1985.

Raynor report recommendations

The features of computerisation for the system were as follows:

- a dispersed series of stand-alone systems in each regional office;
- the main functions to benefit passport writing and searching;
- implementation should be phased over two years;
- data input should be by clerical not specialist data staff;
- the use of Automatic Data Processing (ADP) techniques should be extended to other areas of passport issuing such as examining passports before issuing them;
- the ADP system should be as simple and straightforward as possible to minimise costs and ease acceptance by both management and staff.

Your task

You will be assuming a role for this exercise and will use your brief to analyse the issue of change using new technology.

Section 5 · Financial services

15 · Credit Grantors plc

Bill Richardson and Roy Richardson

This case study has been written from general experience and is intended as an aid to class discussion rather than as a comment on the effectiveness of the handling of a business situation.

Credit Grantors plc is a national finance company and member of the Finance Houses Association. It has a network of branches situated in many of the major towns and cities of England and generates its multi-million pounds annual turnover from the provision of finance in the form of secured and unsecured personal loans. Most business is effected through either of the following strategies:

1. Money shops, forming part of the town/city offices and dealing largely in loans to consumers.
2. Sales representatives ('fieldmen') who are each allocated a sales 'patch' and who generate business through personal selling. This business is, generally, of two types, ie consumer credit sold through trade customers, eg car sales outlets, and industrial credit sold to business customers for industrial investment purposes, eg the purchase of machinery.

Performance appraisal/Management by Objectives

A variation of Management by Objectives is operated by the organisation. Before the start of each financial year individual 'fieldmen' meet with their branch manager and agree monthly targets for the next financial year. A starting point for negotiations is usually the performance achieved during the equivalent periods for the preceding year. Improved but realistic targets usually result from these meetings – it is generally agreed to be in the interests of both the sales representatives and the branch manager (who has to negotiate a branch target with his superior) to set targets which in the event will enable successful performance to be recorded. If agreement cannot be achieved, however, appeal can be made to the area manager. This procedure is rarely used.

Every month (about ten days after the month end) a 'Fieldmen's Performance' list is received from Head Office showing each branch representative's performance against target for that month. Appendix 15.1 shows a copy of such a document relating to performance of staff at Credit

Grantor's Reading branch. The practice is to exhibit the most recent list on the staff notice board.

During the course of each month Head Office also forwards 10-day and 20-day progress reports which the branch manager communicates to all staff (collectively in connection with total branch performance but individually at the initiation of the manager or the individual concerned in connection with individual performance). Staff tend to keep their own progress records as they transact business.

Bonuses attached to performance are not paid although performance levels achieved do form part of the negotiation process at the end of each year when salary changes are negotiated by each representative and the branch manager. Representatives do not receive information on the amount of each other's salary and, between themselves, prefer to remain secretive on this issue.

Appendix 15.1 *Credit Grantors plc – Reading Office*
Performance appraisal
Fieldmen's performance to end August 1992

Name	Margin target £	Performance £	%
AC Crawshaw	5,833	9,662	166
D Fielding	5,600	8,067	143
R Brooksbanks	4,666	6,671	143
J Lodge	6,800	9,662	142
DV Raymond	6,800	7,414	109
LA Fields	6,333	6,429	102
N Kramer	6,250	5,911	95
R Butley	3,583	3,352	94
W Finsher	8,533	7,706	90
JK Robertson	7,500	6,155	82
D Newton	8,950	7,246	81
RI Jameson	9,483	7,382	78
J Cotton	6,675	4,401	66
V Spedding	8,750	5,371	61
R Johnson	6,990	4,010	57
LJ Craven	6,250	3,070	49
PR Tait	6,670	2,237	34
J Lewis	6,670	2,124	32

Section 6 · Industrial products

16 · The attempted takeover of Pilkington by BTR

Claire Capon

Pilkington Brothers was established in 1826 and is still headed by a member of the Pilkington family, Mr Antony Pilkington, who took over as the chairman in 1980.

Whilst enjoying a reputation as a paternalistic employer Pilkington is one of the world's largest producers of glass and related products. Pilkington's products include flat glass, safety glass for car and aircraft windscreens, glass and plastic ophthalmic products, electro-optical systems, insulation products, eg fibre glass, mineral fibres and plastics, and they also supply products to the medical profession and defence industries (see Appendices 16.1(a) and (b)).

In 1986, Pilkington was an international group with one hundred subsidiary companies in 35 countries. In 1986, the group had a turnover of £1,300m and pre-tax profits of £105.8m, about 70 per cent of which was earned outside the UK.

Pilkington's recent long-term strategy

From 1979, Pilkington's long-term strategy was aimed at consolidating world leadership in the glass industry which had become increasingly global and mature. In 1986 Pilkington had 20 per cent of the world market with its nearest rival some 3 per cent behind.

Pilkington expanded in Europe, treated Europe as its home market and then expanded and diversified in America (see p. 156). Considerable time and management effort at Pilkington was also spent 'acquiring marketing skills'.

The strategy was carried out in hostile circumstances as the onset of the European recession in 1979 had plunged the European glass industry into overcapacity and profits had suffered as a result of redundancy costs (see Appendix 16.2). This strategy was executed to ensure that Pilkington survived, despite the maturity of the glass industry, which is illustrated by the fact that Pilkington's royalty income from the float glass production process had been declining as the licences to manufacture float glass expired. The float process which is now the universal method for making high quality flat glass, was developed by Pilkington in the 1950s. Pilkington has continued to invest in large float glass plants, acquiring Flachglas of West Germany and Libbey-Owens-Ford (LOF) of the USA. Flachglas and LOF were both under licence from Pilkington when acquired by Pilkington (see below). An alternative strategy was to invest in small plants, geared to narrower customer needs with lower overheads and a faster stock turnover.

Since 1980, Pilkington's sales have risen steadily and more than doubled from £629m in 1980 to £1321.1m in 1986. However, despite this, pre-tax profit had not risen proportionately, fluctuating from £91.4m in 1980 to £105.8m in 1986, peaking at £116m in 1985 (see Appendix16.2).

The manufacture of glass and planning its production

The manufacture of flat glass is a long-term, large-scale continuous process. A plant to manufacture flat glass can take a year to plan, two years to build and cost between £50m to £100m. Once built such a plant must run efficiently for 24 hours a day, every day, for up to ten years and cannot be turned on and off to meet short-term change in demand.

Therefore, to be successful it is vital that expertise in long-term planning and understanding of markets is used for strategic decisions will have major repercussions for years to come. It is also important that short-term decisions are made with long-term worldwide strategic issues in mind and that decisions made in one subsidiary in one part of the world are made with the rest of the group in mind.

The expansion of Pilkington

Pilkington had continually expanded in Europe and Scandinavia since Britain's entry to the EEC in 1973. In 1980 Pilkington paid £141m for a majority stake in Flachglas, one of West Germany's two large producers of flat glass. At the same time, Pilkington was interested in buying a Benelux and a French company. However, the German Cartel Office intervened and the companies went to Japanese and American interests respectively.

From 1979, the European recession and the arrival of America's Guardian Industries in the European glass industry resulted in a large overcapacity in the European glass market. Pilkington took steps to lower its overcapacity and also increased productivity, but was constantly drained by expensive redundancy costs (Appendix 16.2).

Pilkington has also expanded in the USA. This planned expansion gained pace after 1983 when Pilkington paid £75m for a 30 per cent stake in the Ohio-based conglomerate Libbey-Owens-Ford, taking full control of the glass-making interests of LOF in April 1986. This takeover was the result of a complex $250m deal and increased Pilkington's share of the world's glass market.

Libbey-Owens-Ford, like Pilkington, was originally an old-established glass-making company, established in 1888 in Toledo in the USA. LOF is the world's largest manufacturer of automotive glass and a major supplier of flat glass products to the architectural, mirror and furniture markets, mostly in North America. LOF has been responsible for breakthroughs in Thermopane insulating glass, curved, wrap-around and shaded windscreens, heated backlights and thinner, lighter, safer, automotive glass. It was one of the companies which produced float glass under licence from Pilkington.

The acquisition of Flachglas gave Pilkington a secure base in Europe in a country with a successful and stable economy. The acquisition of these two companies placed Pilkington in a strong position to serve the world's car manufacturers, including the opportunity to enter into a number of joint ventures with a Japanese glass-maker to supply the Japanese car industry as it expands overseas.

Pilkington's expansion into the USA continued with the acquisition of smaller companies including in mid-November 1986, the takeover, at a cost of £42m, of the Arizona-based Syntex Ophthalmic, which makes contact lenses.

It has been said that Pilkington had followed a 'textbook strategy', but maybe it started changing later than it should. In 1986, Pilkington looked an attractive acquisition prospect to BTR...

BTR

BTR is an industrial conglomerate, which began its modern development some 20 years ago and has since been built up into one of Britain's 'biggest and most aggressive industrial groups, with a remarkable appetite for swallowing less efficient businesses'. BTR is run from 'spartan headquarters in London's Pimlico district'.

In 1986, Sir Owen Green, the 61-year-old chairman of BTR, was described as 'having an open, cheery and down-to-earth manner and a rapid way of speaking that suggests a highly active mind'. He is an accountant by training and has been managing director of BTR since 1967.

In 1986, BTR owned companies in the areas of the construction industry, the energy and electrical industry, health care, paper and printing, transportation, plus other related holdings. These diverse interests resulted in a wide variety of products which included industrial hose, car wheels, and 'Pretty Polly' tights.

BTR has expanded by buying companies in a poor position, improving their performance and enhancing profitability. Such companies as Dunlop and Thomas Tilling were related to BTR's core operations (see Appendix 16.3).

BTR's policy of acquisition is ideally illustrated by the case of Dunlop which was successfully turned around by BTR. Dunlop was taken over by BTR in 1984 and two years later Dunlop was thriving under BTR's ownership. Profits and levels of capital investment had both risen sharply. BTR paid minute attention to profits in the short term to achieve success. Hence the rigorous system of financial control proved to be a vigorous and disciplined way of controlling operations. These control factors have been a crucial factor in the growth of BTR whose profits rose from £24m in 1976 to £362m in 1985. Pilkington has gone from near financial collapse in the 1950s to profits for 1986 of £105.8m (see Appendix 16.2).

At the end of November 1986, BTR launched a £1,160m takeover bid for Pilkington because, BTR argued, the two companies shared similar markets. Pilkington's business served the construction, transport and health care industries in which BTR also had a substantial presence. Both companies also had interests in Europe, Australia and the USA.

The success of such a bid would have altered BTR's shape, with the total assets less current liabilities figure more than doubling for BTR, based on 1985 figures. BTR in 1985 was approximately three times the size of Pilkington in terms of revenue, therefore success for BTR would have resulted in about 25 per cent of BTR's turnover coming from glass and related products (see Appendices 16.2 and 16.4).

The BTR bid

In November 1986, BTR launched a £1,160m takeover bid for Pilkington. When this occurred, Pilkington regarded the bid as hostile claiming that absorption into an industrial conglomerate like BTR would prejudice their international position. The glass industry is an industry with long lead times and heavy research and development expenditure, and Pilkington regarded industrial conglomerates as tending to take a short-term view.

The Financial Times described the takeover battle as 'a classic clash of corporate cultures', between BTR, a diversified industrial conglomerate with a reputation for successful takeovers, and Pilkington which was seen as an old, successful, well-run manufacturing company on a recovery track and not closely related to the core operations of BTR.

BTR had, by the end of November 1986, built up a 3.8 per cent stake in Pilkington, through an associate's share buying which began on 4 September 1986. Before 4 September 1986, Pilkington's share price stood at 428p. The news that BTR were to launch a takeover bid sent Pilkington's share price from 530p to 611p, far above BTR's offer price of 544p which was based on the value of BTR shares, 291p, down 3p on the day the bid was announced.

Pilkington's defence plan

Pilkington's defence plan had two main elements:

1   profit expectations for 1987, which surprised both BTR and the City when they were revealed at the appropriate time towards the end of the bid's run; and
2   Pilkington's claim that it had a coherent business strategy, which it sought to demonstrate.

Pilkington argued that although it had licensed the float process which could have given it a technological advantage, it was capable of maintaining its leadership in the glass business by adding value to its basic products, flat and safety glass. In 1986 about 70 per cent of Pilkington's sales resulted from value-added products, other than basic glass.

A similar argument applied to Pilkington's business with the world's car industry, in supplying automotive glass. Pilkington was supplying glass to the US car industry, including 65 per cent of the safety glass used in General Motors' vehicles. Pilkington also had joint ventures to supply Japanese car makers with automotive glass, as well as a stable base in Europe with Flachglas of West Germany, PFAB in Sweden, Lamino in Finland and Pilkington Glass Limited in the UK.

Pilkington had also moved into areas of new technology, ophthalmics and electro-optics, which involved supplying defence, medical equipment and aerospace companies.

Pilkington issued to shareholders a defence document which made a number of points:

1   It was expected that a dividend of 22p for 1987 would be paid, compared to 13.5p for 1986.
2   It was necessary to invest in research and development, as a failure to do so would result in a lack of new developments and technology and hence an erosion of company competitiveness.
3   Pilkington dismissed BTR's claim that the two companies shared similar markets, by claiming that as BTR's business was so diverse it was inevitable that they should serve industries such as construction, transport and health care in which Pilkington and many other companies also operated.
4   Pilkington claimed that BTR was not able to state how the short-term improvements in performance would be obtained and also claimed long-term detrimental effects on Pilkington's business of the measures BTR proposed to implement should the bid be successful.

Four of the seven full-time executives from the Pilkington board moved to London full-time to fight the bid, and the company also took the relatively unusual step, of appointing an extremely strong team of advisers including two public relations companies.

The bid's progress and issues raised

Research and development

One of the major issues in the takeover battle between Pilkington and BTR was the extent of commitment to research and development demonstrated by each company.

The commitment of Pilkington to research and development has always been regarded as being strong, particularly since the development of the float process. Since its invention Pilkington has continued to invest approximately £30m a year in the float process, approximately half its total research and development budget of over £50m. Licensing and technical fees earn Pilkington about £30m a year from the float process.

The geographical diversification of sales has taken place in parallel with the diversification of research and development facilities. In the late 1970s, all of Pilkington's research and development was concentrated at a central research laboratory in Latham in Lancashire. In 1986 about 70 per cent of the research and development budget was spent by divisions and only 30 per cent in the central laboratories.

Pilkington regarded the value of central research and development as important. Scientists at the central laboratories were seen as responsible for keeping close to and up with the science that might suddenly become commercially important, although there must be close interaction between divisional and central scientists.

BTR's apparent lack of commitment to research and development and lack of a central research and development laboratory could be regarded as reflecting BTR's short-term approach to business, claimed Pilkington. However, parts of the BTR conglomerate have a greater commitment to research and development, most notably the aerospace companies, mostly acquired with the takeover of Dunlop and Thomas Tilling.

BTR's approach to research and development was to have individual 'centres of excellence' where they were needed and appropriate to the market they serve. BTR did not see a need to put research and development in the forefront of the group's activities, but to place research and development where it appeared to be required with the funding it needed.

Unions

An unusual factor in the case of the attempted takeover of Pilkington by BTR was the involvement of the trade unions at Pilkington and the local St Helens community.

The rallying round of the local community stems from two main factors:

1   Pilkington's involvement in St Helens in terms of social effort; and
2   the fact that Pilkington has kept its world headquarters in St Helens.

At a meeting on 7 January 1987, union representatives for the 16,500 Pilkington employees in the UK, union representatives from Pilkington-Flachglas in West Germany and two worker-directors from Pilkington's Swedish subsidiary gave their unanimous support to Pilkington in resisting the takeover bid. This support from the unions was a direct result of Pilkington's style of management and industrial relations policies which centred on achieving co-operation with the unions.

External organised lobbying of MPs, Government ministers, and major shareholders was undertaken, and resulting all party parliamentary support was extensive. The first stage of the lobbying was an attempt to persuade the Office of Fair Trading and Mr Paul Channon, Trade and Industry Secretary, that the bid should be referred to the Monopolies and Mergers Commission, on the grounds that BTR was an aggressively acquisitive industrial conglomerate, which placed a strong emphasis on short-term performance, while Pilkington was an important regional employer in north-west England with a strong commitment to research and development.

The second stage of the campaign was directed at 18 financial institutions and Pilkington's other major institutional shareholders.

The General Municipal and Boilermakers' Union broke new ground in the takeover battle, when it wrote to members who were pension fund trustees urging them to take an active role in deciding whether the pension funds should accept the BTR bid.

The Monopolies Commission

On 14 January 1987, Pilkington shares rose 20p to close at 651p, amid rumours that the bid was not going to be referred to the Monopolies and Mergers Commission. On 15 January 1987, the Government announced the decision not to refer the takeover bid to the Commission. This decision was taken because the merger did not raise significant competition issues. In making this statement, Mr Paul Channon referred to the 1984 Government Statement on monopolies which stated that the primary yardstick for a monopolies reference should be competition. BTR has no existing interests in the glass industry.

The decision not to refer the bid to the MMC caused Pilkington's share price to rise by 34p to 685p. It was reported that three Ministers of State at the Department of Trade and Industry, Mr Giles Shaw, Mr Geoffrey Pattie and Mr Alan Clark did not approve of the Government's decision not to refer the bid. It was further claimed that a substantial number of Tory MPs also disapproved of this decision.

Pilkington's ace

On 16 January 1987, Pilkington announced expected pre-tax profits of £250m, more than double the previous year's profits. All parts of Pilkington were expected to do well. The forecast of such good results for Pilkington was used to reinforce the success of Pilkington's long-term strategy.

Highlights of the forecast included the following:

1 All parts of the business were expected to outperform 1986's results, with particularly strong improvements in Britain and mainland Europe, where profits were expected to be up by about 300 per cent.
2 In Britain the profit forecast was £73m helped by better prices and a marked turn around in the glass fibres division which only two years previously was breaking even (see Appendices 16.1(a) and (b)).

3 A 67 per cent rise in sales from £1.3bn to £2.2bn, with £600m from consolidation of subsidiary figures, which included £15m from Libbey-Owens-Ford. Approximately £200m came from growth of existing business, up 15 per cent.

4 At the trading level, Pilkington forecast a rise of 125 per cent after redundancy costs which were to be halved at £11m, trading profits were put at £234m.

This forecast caused Pilkington's share price to rise by 25p to 710p. The BTR offer was 542p.

The outcome

On 20 January 1987, BTR abandoned its bid for Pilkington Brothers. The following reasons were given by BTR for the decision to withdraw the bid:

1 Pilkington's forecast of profits for 1986–87 and widely discussed estimates for 1987–88 profits;
2 the short- and long-term effect of unusually aggressive price increases; and
3 advice on the price at which major institutions would sell their holdings.

The conclusion of BTR was that the revision necessary for a bid to have succeeded would have involved a price for a cyclical business, greater than any which would have been in the best interests of BTR shareholders.

Sir Owen Green stated that BTR intended to hold on to the 3.8 per cent stake in Pilkington which it had built up before the launching of the bid. The upward trend in Pilkington's share price throughout the bid meant BTR was showing a paper profit of about £16m, enough to cover its costs in the battle.

The lapsing of the bid hit Pilkington's share price, it closed at 610p, down 35p on the day and 50p below the 710p share price reached on the day Pilkington announced their expected results for 1986–87.

BTR's share price continued its downward trend and closed down 1p at 288p.

Sir Anthony Pilkington expressed delight at the victory.

Supplementary note 1

In the event, Pilkington met its profit promise for 1986–87 with pre-tax profits of £256m, some £6m more than the January estimate.

Pilkington's results for 1987 (1986) were:

Sales	£2103.4m	(£1321.0m)
Group profit before tax	£256.0m	(£123.3m)
Earnings per share	73.1p	(22.2p)

Pilkington argued that the profit figure would have been higher had it not been for adverse movements in the exchange rate, and claimed:

'the beneficial effects of restructuring are now evident ... better geographical balance, higher productivity and firmer prices have all contributed to the acceleration of the Group's profitability.'

A few days after the announcement, Pilkington's share price stood at 947p.

Supplementary note 2

Pilkington intends that the products it produces will always be related to glass.

By the early 1990s, Pilkington sees itself as being in the flat and safety glass business, producing high value-added products. It expects to lead the way in the innovation of coated glasses, and in products such as glass subsystems for cars. The new technology products manufactured by Pilkington include communications systems using fibre optic cables, which cannot be tapped in the way that copper cables can.

In 1987, Pilkington held approximately 20 per cent of the market for plastic lenses, placing it 7th/8th in the whole ophthalmics market. Pilkington expects to expand in the ophthalmic market by producing more ophthalmic products, including the manufacture of a new type of bifocal contact lens, using holographic technology.

Appendix 16.1(a) *Contribution by product type to total sales and profit/(loss) as calculated on replacement cost basis*[1]

	Sales (£m)				Trading profit/(loss) (£m)			
	1983	*1984*	*1985*	*1986*	*1983*	*1984*	*1985*	*1986*
Flat and safety glass	898.2	1134.8	1089.6	1140.6	58.7	82.6	82.9	60.8
Ophthalmic	58.5	71.9	82.7	98.7	(1.1)	1.3	4.3	7.6
Electro optics	62.5	75.2	81.3	91.6	6.4	6.6	7.4	7.1
Glass fibres	131.0	136.0	151.1	162.9	(14.8)	(6.0)	(1.8)	1.9
New ventures	2.2	3.6	5.5	10.2	(2.0)	(2.0)	(2.9)	(4.5)
Group expenditure and service companies	2.7	3.1	3.8	6.6	(6.2)	(5.8)	(3.1)	(4.7)
	1155.1	1424.6	1414.0	1510.6	41.0	76.7	86.8	68.2
Less: sales to group companies	133.5	210.2	187.1	189.5	–	–	–	–
	1021.6	1214.4	1226.9	1321.1	41.0	76.7	86.8	68.2

Note: [1]Replacement cost basis: the value of assets which appears on the balance sheet is estimated to be the amount at which the assets could currently be replaced. Pilkington have recently changed to using a historical cost basis, which values assets at actual past money cost.

Source: Pilkington Annual Reports 1984–86

Appendix 16.1(b) *Percentage contribution by product type to total sales and profit/(loss) as calculated on replacement cost sales*[1]

	Sales				Trading profit/(loss)			
	1983	1984	1985	1986	1983	1984	1985	1986
Flat and safety glass	77.8	79.65	77	75.5	143.2	107.7	95.5	89.15
Ophthalmic	5.1	5.05	5.85	6.5	(2.7)	1.7	4.9	11.15
Electro optics	5.4	5.3	5.75	6.1	15.6	8.6	8.5	10.4
Glass fibres	11.3	9.55	10.7	10.8	(36.1)	(7.8)	(2)	2.8
New ventures	0.2	0.25	0.4	0.7	(4.9)	(2.6)	(3.3)	(6.6)
Group expenditure and service companies	0.2	0.2	0.3	0.4	(15.1)	(7.6)	(3.6)	(6.9)
	100	100	100	100	100	100	100	100
Less: sales to group companies	11.6	14.75	13.2	12.5	–	–	–	–
	88.4	85.25	86.8	87.5				
Index of growth	100	119	120	129	100	187	212	166

Note: [1]For explanation, see Appendix 16.1(a)
Source: Calculated from Appendix 16.1(a)

Appendix 16.2 *Key financial record for Pilkington as calculated on replacement cost basis*[1]

	1980 £m	1981 £m	1982 £m	1983 £m	1984 £m	1985 £m	1986 £m
Sales	629.0	768.8	958.9	1021.6	1214.4	1226.9	1321.1
Profits							
Group profits before redundancy adjustment	u	u	74.7	64.6	103.8	125.6	126.9
Redundancy adjustment	u	u	21.3	14.7	15.5	9.6	21.1
Group profit before taxation	91.4	81.0	53.4	49.9	88.3	116.0	105.8
Group profit after taxation	70.9	48.8	3.5	8.9	36.7	51.7	44.6
Assets							
Tangible assets	455.3	852.0	924.7	1016.5	1097.6	1105.1	1103.3
Total assets less current liabilities	759.7	1157.5	1219.0	1421.5	1523.3	1625.3	1574.1
Net current assets	263.4	244.9	223.7	254.4	259.3	334.1	258.2
Financed by							
Total capital and reserves	581.9	736.1	791.7	865.8	898.6	1040.7	997.6
Minority interest and loan capital	117.8	421.4	427.3	555.7	663.7	584.6	576.5
Key figures							
Trading profit to sales	7.8%	6.1%	2.8%	4.0%	6.3%	7.1%	5.2%
Earnings per share (restated to take account of rights issue) before extraordinary items	52.0p	24.6p	(3.7p)	2.3p	13.3p	21.8p	15.3p

Note: [1] for explanation, see Appendix 16.1(a)
        u = unknown
Source: Pilkington Annual Reports 1984–86

Appendix 16.3 *The rise of BTR*

Date	Target	Field	Price
March 1985	Dunlop	Tyre and rubber products	£101m
June 1983	Thomas Tilling	Construction, publishing, health care	£700m
Dec. 1981	Serck	Valve manufacturing	£24m
Sept. 1980	Huyck Corp. (US)	Paper-making equipment	£65m
Aug. 1978	Worcester Controls Corp. (US)	Valve manufacturer	£25m
Dec. 1977	Allied Polymer	Rubber and plastics	£9.5m
June 1977	Andre Silentbloc	Rubber products manufacturing	£6m
Recent Disposals			
Jan. 1986	Cornhill Insurance	Insurance	£305m
Aug. 1985	Heinemann	Publishing	£100m

Source: *The Financial Times*, 21 November 1986

Appendix 16.4 *Key financial record for BTR as calculated on historical cost basis*[1]

	1976 £m	1977 £m	1978 £m	1979 £m	1980 £m	1981 £m	1982 £m	1983 £m	1984 £m	1985 £m
Sales	212	248	351	433	510	638	725	1970	3487	3881
Profit before taxation	24	30	40	57	70	90	107	171	284	362
Assets										
Fixed assets	65	74	114	124	220	285	301	838	901	1030
Net trading assets (net current assets)	35	32	68	67	83	118	141	526	556	891
Financed by										
Shareholders interests	56	81	135	149	222	261	317	692	847	1016
Total funds (including shareholders funds)	100	106	182	191	303	403	442	1364	1457	1921
Earnings per BTR share	13p	18p	23p	32p	43p	57p	69p	113p	194p	261p

Note: [1]For explanation, see Appendix 16.1(a)
Source: BTR Annual Report 1985

Appendix 16.5 *Pilkington: geographical diversification of sales*

| | Percentage of Sales | |
	1986	Late 1970s
UK	25	61
Europe	29	11
USA	26	1
Other	20	27

Source: The Financial Times, 20 February 1987

17 · Redlake Forge Ltd

John Patterson and Susan Leeson

Redlake Forge Ltd, a profitable and diversified engineering company, manufactures a range of machine tools for the food processing industry. For a résumé of the firm's history see Appendix 17.1.

A mainstay of Redlake's current range is a manually operated fish filleting machine used in the preparation of fish fingers and uniform sized fillets. This machine is in wide use by such companies as Bird's Eye Foods and Findus. End-users, however, are actively looking for ways of further automating their production processes and Redlake is consequently worried as to the future marketability of its current product.

The company's research manager has learned of a newly patented fish filleting machine which is computer controlled and quickly enables different fillet sizes to be introduced into the production line. Not only is fillet time reduced but trial runs have indicated that fish waste is halved.

This patent can be purchased for £120,000, but to enable Redlake to produce the new machine, considerable modifications would be required to its manufacturing facilities in order to incorporate the electronic control mechanisms; it is thought that these modifications will cost £80,000.

Such modifications are not expected to affect the remaining four-year life of the plant and equipment nor its anticipated scrap value of £20,000. Although fixed costs other than depreciation charges will be unaffected variable costs per filleting machine will increase by an expected £1,000. If the new machine is produced, production of the current machine will have to cease.

Other information

(a) The marketing manager thinks that a competitor is also interested in buying the patent, and that if it does then Redlake's sales of its current filleting machine will fall from 200 units to about 120 units per year. However, if the patent is purchased by Redlake and the selling price held the marketing manager feels that the increase in market share could result in sales of up to 380 units per year.

The current product has been established for so long that end-users routinely replace it each year, thus, advertising and promotion has been reduced to £10,000 per year (included in fixed costs).

The company does not export but the marketing manager has researched the likely effects of 1992 and believes that with the harmonisation of technical standards there may be a market for up to 130 units in West Germany. However, this would only be for the final two years of the expected product life. A German import agency could be contracted for about £25,000 a year. Extra packaging and transport variable costs on exported machines would increase by a further £100. The manager admits that there is a high degree of uncertainty in this possible outlet.

(b) The research manager feels that because of the pace of technical change it would be unwise to put an economic life of more than four years on the new machine; after this period the patent will be virtually worthless.

(c) The senior engineer thinks he can ensure that the plant modifications can be completed in the shutdown over Xmas ready for start up in the new year.

(d) There is some dispute among the production managers. The senior manager is confident that there will be no production run problems whereas his two line foremen are worried about the extreme close tolerance standards required by the new machine. They believe that in the first six months direct costs could be 25 per cent greater than estimated. The senior manager rejects this view.

(e) The income and expenses statement for the current machine is summarised below (includes £40,000 depreciation charge):

Sales (200 pa @ £4000 per unit)	£800,000
Variable costs	£450,000
Fixed costs	£240,000
Net income	£110,000

(f) The company's minimum rate of return on investment is 22 per cent.

(g) If the change is made the increased level of production would raise working capital requirement from its present £10,000 to £20,000 due to higher inventory needs.

(h) The current corporation tax rate is 35 per cent (although the business press is suggesting that the Chancellor may reduce it to 30 per cent in next year's budget). As with most companies Redlake pays its tax liability one year in arrears.

(i) Investment in plant and equipment can be written off against tax liability on a reducing balance basis at 25 per cent pa for eight years or the holding period of the asset(s) if less.

(j) For tax depreciation purposes the purchase of the patent can be treated in the same way as (i) above.

(k) Although the company's required rate of return on investment is 22 per cent, this is 7 per cent above the company's actual cost of capital. If the investment is approved the company will raise a medium-term bank loan to be repaid at the end of five years.

(l) Trade data for the past twenty years on equipment investment by the food processing industry is given below in constant 1970 £m. Note that the dip

in expenditure in 1974/75 and 1981 to 1983 occurred in years of recession
and high interest rates.

1970	1971	1972	1973	1974	1975	1976	1977	1978
£18	£20	£25	£23	£16	£17	£22	£26	£29

1979	1980	1981	1982	1983	1984	1985	1986	1987
£30	£28	£20	£18	£22	£29	£32	£34	£33

1988	1989
£36	£36

(m) The marketing manager has produced the following data from a 1989
MINTEL report:

Fish consumption by type and volume 1984–88

	1984 %	1985 %	1986 %	1987 %	1988 %
Fresh fish	28	28	28	27	28
Frozen convenience packets	21	21	20	19	19
Canned	14	14	16	18	18
Cooked	14	12	12	12	13
Frozen fillets	11	13	12	12	12
Processed	8	8	8	7	7
Shellfish	3	3	3	3	3

Forecast sales of fish at 1989 prices 1990–94

	£m Fresh	£m Frozen	£m Convenience	£m Shell
1990	448	207	775	110
1991	473	209	776	106
1992	478	212	792	108
1993	481	211	795	113
1994	489	213	800	113

The food processing industry is becoming increasingly automated and the new
fish stripping machine is evidence that processing technology is rapidly
changing. The new machine is complex in that it requires several finely
machined components constructed of a number of metals and alloys such as
stainless steel and manganese steel as well as the integrated circuitry associated
with CNC tools. Whilst its fabrication is not beyond the capabilities of Redlake
the tighter tolerances will necessitate the installation of more sophisticated
manufacturing tools and equipment. Other requirements would be the

acquisition of personnel skilled in electronic assembly and testing, or alternatively sub-contracting this element to an outside firm. The estimated increase in staff for the new machine is 2 fitters, 2 turners, and 2 instrument/electronic technicians. This addition to the labour force should be able to cope with an annual output level of about 400 units without having a detrimental effect on the company's mainstream business.

The present breakdown of staffing below the management level is as follows:

```
 2   staff, 1 progress chaser, and 1 stock controller
15   sheet metal workers
12   engineering fitters
 6   welders
 4   turners
 4   electrical fitters
 4   burners
 1   carpenter
10   general craftsmen's labourers
 1   storekeeper
```

In addition there are 2 office clerk/typists and a cleaner.

Appendix 17.1 *Redlake Forge Ltd: background*

The company was established in 1958 by eight skilled craftsmen, all hitherto employed in engineering trades in the Humber shipbuilding and repair industry. Following the decline of the industry the men decided to pool their redundancy payments and personal savings to set up an engineering repair business to service the booming new manufacturing industries locating on the Humber Bank.

Redlake began operating from some run-down premises between the rail yard and the fish docks. Though still working from the same site today the premises have been much improved, for example by the addition of a materials stockyard, a fabricating shop, and a machining shop. With the almost complete decline of the fish docks and associated rail yards there is no shortage of development land, although the region does not qualify for development aid.

Fortunately for the founders the decline of traditional ship-related engineering coincided with the growth of the frozen food industry stimulated by the launch of the now ubiquitous fish finger in the late 1950s. The area is now Europe's major centre for frozen food manufacturing and contains household names such as the Ross Group, Bird's Eye Foods, Findus, Christian Salvesen, and Northern Foods who are own brand suppliers to multiples such as Marks & Spencer.

Such a rapid growth required skilled engineering satellite companies and Redlake, because of its strong engineering base, was a major beneficiary. Steady, if unspectacular, growth took place from the early 1960s to the present, and the company now has recognised expertise in on- and off-site maintenance and the fabrication of original equipment on a job-order basis (although the main focus is still maintenance work). Redlake has a long-established reputation for prompt, high quality work and a sound customer base spread across all the food processors.

As a result of this growth the original partnership was changed in 1970 into a private limited company. Between 1980 and 1987 three of the founder members retired but still take an active interest by retaining their shareholding and as non-executive directors. Because of the structure of ownership, all previous development, eg the construction of the fabricating shop, has been funded by medium-term bank loans. The shares are concentrated within the original families who will not countenance dilution by bringing in outside equity capital.

In 1965 the company was asked to manufacture a manually operated fish-stripping machine which proved well within its engineering capabilities, and from this developed the current filleter. Today the manufacture of this machine involves about 20 per cent of the workforce. The works operates as a jobbing shop and a large proportion of the staple maintenance work is done on-site at the food processors.

By 1989 Redlake had a workforce of 60, a low labour turnover (8 per cent), and each year took on four apprentices, one each in sheet metal working, welding, turning and fitting. The workforce is best described as comprising flexible but not multi-skilled craftsmen; this flexibility extends to both production and maintenance work as well as on- and off-site work. The origins of the company mean that an 'us and them' attitude between management and the shopfloor has never been allowed to develop, and all workers are encouraged to join the main engineering union.

The company employs no personnel of professional standing, the founders developed hands-on management skills and as the business grew took over functional responsibilities in areas recognised as 'Production and Workshop Manager', 'Office Manager/Accountant', 'Sales and Marketing' and 'Research'.

18 · NAM UK

Susan Leeson and Anthea Gregory

NAM UK is the UK arm of North American Metals, a large producer of steel in the USA. The following is a brief history of NAM UK.

1964: The UK business is established to stockhold and distribute the parent company's high grade steel.

1966: Mould steel for the plastics industry is attached to the UK company's product portfolio.

1967: The exchange rate deteriorates seriously and it becomes no longer viable for NAM UK to source its product range from the US parent company. Company strategy is changed and NAM UK is given total freedom to source its business.

1968: The parent company is taken over by a very large US corporation but the change of ownership has little effect on the UK business operation.

1973: Tubes and pipes from the US parent company are attached to NAM UK's product offering. The exchange rate soon damages this strategy resulting in NAM UK again having to source this new product from elsewhere.

1980: A new chairman takes control of the group heralding the beginning of an expansionist era.

New products are attached to the portfolio such as pipe fittings, pipe flanges and a new range of pipes which could be sold to the company's existing markets. NAM UK's inventories increase, sales personnel increase in number, the company's market share increases and the enthusiastic and expansionist attitude of the US chairman filters through the entire company.

NAM UK senior staff

Peter Black, managing director

Peter Black left grammar school with 8 'O' levels and 3 'A' levels. At the age of 18 he joined Union Carbide's cost accounting department where he worked for two years as a trainee accountant. Wishing to broaden his accountancy experience he then joined a finance company to take up a post in financial accounting. He studied for his accountancy exams on a day release basis and became chartered at the age of 22. In 1969 at the age of 23 he successfully applied for the post of chief accountant at NAM UK, a position he held for seven years. Then after three years as company secretary he became managing director of NAM UK.

Peter married in the year of his accountancy finals. Up until the birth of his children he had a successful athletics 'career' as a sprinter on the northern amateur circuit. His recreation is now family centred.

John Malpass, sales and marketing manager

John Malpass was born in 1933 and educated at grammar school; he entered the RAF on a ten-year contract and on its completion joined the sales and marketing department of a major Swedish steel company. This company has always been renowned for its professionalism and the quality of training which it gives its staff. On joining the company John was encouraged to study for qualifications, which he did at night class, gaining a Higher National in metallurgy.

In 1975 he joined NAM UK as product manager of the stainless operation; later he took on tool steel operations and was made head of sales and marketing by Peter Black early in 1985.

Peter Black describes him as very energetic and a mine of information, 'He knows who's who in the world of steel and who has taken over who. He has a very professional attitude to the job. If he doesn't want to retire at 65 I'll be pleased for him to stay on.'

John is married. His children have grown up and left home and his hobbies are best described as gardening and eating out.

David Harris, company secretary

David Harris is a local man. He was an undergraduate in economics at Liverpool University but left the course preferring to work and study part-time for qualifications in accountancy.

After practising accountancy for 15 years he joined NAM UK in 1979 as company secretary.

He is married with a family. His hobby is motor sports.

June 1991

Peter Black calls a meeting of his senior colleagues to report on his corporate visit to NAM in the United States and to outline the basic strategy which the main board believe the UK operation should follow. After opening the meeting he continues.

'As you know the 1980s heralded an expansionist attitude. Up until then we had been starved of capital for projects but with the takeover of the present company and the appointment of a new chairman funds were made available to us and our overdraft facilities were increased.

'Since the company's inception we have expanded our product range and the UK company has grown from being a stockholder and distributor of a single product to one which sources and markets a considerable range of high grade steel products. Much of the success of our operation is due to thorough market analysis and good marketing policies.

'Since 1980 we have tripled our return on investment and increased our net worth substantially.

'We are now in a strong position to consider expansion which is in fact necessary if we are to continue our present rate of growth. The strategy which will allow us to create the necessary growth is the main item on our agenda today.

'It has been decided that we are to increase our presence in the plastics moulding business and hence move more strongly into manufacturing as a result.

'As you know our present customers use our steel for making their own moulds, a lengthy machining task, to make a wide variety of products from train seats and vacuum cleaner casings to telephones. The product we intend to manufacture is in fact many thousands of product parts of differing basic shapes which we would machine to the customer's specification. This would mean they wouldn't have to undertake this process themselves; customers would simply refer to our extensive catalogue and create their required mould by piecing together specially ordered components from us. This will be a fast and trouble free way of providing a mould-maker with a mould.

'At this moment in time the UK has only one major player in this field, Pressform of Bristol, though on the Continent there are a number of companies producing similar products: as yet none are exporting to the UK. Pressform has only been in operation since 1980 but it seems to be doing very well so I sent off for its accounts from Companies House and a copy of the information I received is available for your inspection (see Appendix 18.1). In order to put their results into perspective I also managed to get industry average figures from the Steel Products Manufacturers Trade Association (see Appendix 18.2). I realise that financial results from a wide range of manufacturers have been used to give these aggregated figures, but this is the best information available for comparison at present. Further, according to my contacts, Pressform has a considerable waiting list and I know this has been achieved with only negligible marketing. This only adds weight to my conviction that this is the market to expand into.

'The company now has expanded to its limits on this inner-city site and so we would be unable to produce the new product here. We therefore have two options. One is that we could move the entire company's operations to a greenfield site. This would have certain advantages but I think they could be greatly outweighed by the problems we may encounter. Also, this strategy would require considerable investment. Alternatively, as the proposed expansion of operations is to be in a new process (manufacturing not stockholding) and a new product line, we could operate this new venture on a different site.

'We have made enquiries into a site in Calthorpe. Calthorpe is 35 miles east of here and the road connections are of motorway standard. Previously the town was a steel smelting centre but with the downturn in that industry many jobs have been lost. However, the local authorities have lost no time in encouraging diverse industries into the area all of which are now competing for labour. As you know it is a development area and funds are available from both the UK Government and the EC.

'Our initial strategic plan suggested we would require a factory unit on one level of about 10,000 square metres. There are sites available for rent or purchase which would meet that requirement. We must therefore decide what to do. Purchase prices are in the range of £1m whereas rent for an equivalent site would be in the region of £50,000 per annum.

'We have £1.5m finance available to us at an interest rate of 12 per cent in the form of various medium-term loans from the US parent company, the UK Government and the EC. It is the parent company's policy that all investments have a payback period of less than 3 years. It may seem too short a payback period to some people but this criterion must be met otherwise our parent company will not allow the project to go ahead.

'As for equipping the new factory, we have looked at a number of manufacturing equipment suppliers. We have narrowed this down to two makers (Appendix 18.3 gives details of the machines under consideration). Which machines are purchased is a decision we will have to make soon, cost will naturally be a major factor but we must not lose sight of the fact that NAM UK has sold its products on 'service and quality' and neither of these factors can be compromised.

'We must decide what price to charge for the product. We are a quality, not low cost, supplier. However, we must bear in mind the market price; Press form's average list price is £15 per unit but I am aware that they give discounts to customers. I would imagine their cost structure would not be dissimilar to our cost projections (ie, those given in Appendix 18.3). This may help us in setting our prices. We must also consider the shorter term though and decide on a pricing strategy that will ensure our product is accepted in the market.

'Much of what I have had to say so far has assumed that should we take up the Calthorpe option it will run as well as our Head Office operation and to the same high standards of quality and commitment. It would be wrong of us to assume that the choice of manager of the proposed plant will be easy and I think we will require some advice to help us find and select the right candidate.

'There have been a number of CVs sent in (Appendix 18.4 summarises these) so we now need to discuss the ideal candidate for the job.

'I want a manager who has an engineering background, a background of theoretical knowledge coupled with hands-on experience. This person will understand the vital importance of accurate tolerances in this new product as well as the operators' problems.'

JOHN MALPASS: I think we need to be looking at someone with at least an HND in mechanical or electrical engineering, a degree would be useful but not essential. I think this person will have spent say 5–10 years working in and managing a machine shop of some complexity. We certainly don't want someone who has jumped from company to company. Quality, stability and commitment is what we are looking for. The candidate must have been involved in selling, of course. Production types who haven't sold their product never know the true value of producing a quality product.

DAVID HARRIS: I second what you have both said. This manager will need people skills, engineering skills and selling skills, but I suggest we also look for someone who has some financial appreciation, so that he or she might assess the costs, in the broadest terms, of work in progress.

PETER BLACK: This is quite a specification! I would like to reiterate my comment about someone who has a balance between a theoretical background and practical experience and add that this person must have commitment. Starting a new product line and opening a new factory will not be easy. I don't want someone who will give up when the going gets tough, I want a problem-solver. Age, I think, 30–55.

Once the project is off the starting block we will need to look at recruitment, selection and how we should approach training.

Initial research shows that though some major organisations have moved into the area there should not be a problem in attracting a suitable workforce. We have always paid our skilled and committed staff well and given the others opportunities to develop skills if they wanted it; I intend that this policy should be pursued at Calthorpe.

Well, gentlemen, we have much to do and many decisions to take! Can I suggest we make provisional arrangements to meet again to discuss our findings one month from today?

Appendix 18.1(a) *Profit and loss accounts for Pressform of Bristol*

	31.12.88 £000	31.12.89 £000	31.12.90 £000
Turnover	742	854	962
Cost of goods sold	265	299	329
Gross profit	477	555	633
Less operating expenses:			
Marketing, selling and distribution	29	38	40
Administrative expenses	43	49	52
Gross operating income	405	468	541
Depreciation	63	72	80
Net operating income	342	396	461
Less other expenses:			
Interest	35	20	15
Profit before tax	307	376	446

	31.12.88 £000	31.12.89 £000	31.12.90 £000
Corporation tax	96	114	129
Net profit after tax	211	262	317
Dividends	145	170	215
Retained profit for year	66	92	102

Appendix 18.1(b) *Balance Sheet for Pressform of Bristol –*
31 December 1990

	£000	£000
Fixed assets		
Freehold land and buildings		710
Plant and equipment		130
		840
Current assets		
Stock	105	
Debts and prepayments	214	
Quoted investments	226	
Cash and bank balance	143	
	688	
Current liabilities		
Creditors and accruals	330	
Loans	200	
	530	158
		998
Capital and reserves		
Share capital (500,000 £1 ordinary shares)		500
Retained earnings		342
Capital reserve		156
		998

Previous year's turnover

1985 £000	1986 £000	1987 £000
397	582	693

Appendix 18.2 *Industry averages provided by the Steel Manufacturers Trade Association (1990)*

Current ratio	1.2 times
Acid test	1.1 times
Gearing (debt to total assets)	40%
Stock turnover	12 times
Return on net worth	27%
Return on total assets	15%
Average collection period	60 days
Gross profit margin	50%

Formulae used for calculation

Current ratio

$$\frac{\text{Current assets}}{\text{Current liabilities}}$$

Acid test

$$\frac{\text{Current assets} - \text{stock}}{\text{Current liabilities}}$$

Debt to total assets

$$\frac{\text{Total debt}}{\text{Total assets}}$$

Stock turnover

$$\frac{\text{Sales}}{\text{Stock}}$$

Return on net worth

$$\frac{\text{Net profit after tax and interest}}{\text{Net worth}}$$

Return on total assets

$$\frac{\text{Net profit after tax and interest}}{\text{Total assets}}$$

Average collection period

$$\frac{\text{Debtors}}{\text{Sales per day}}$$

Gross profit margin

$$\frac{\text{Gross profit}}{\text{Sales}}$$

Appendix 18.3 *The equipment decision*

There are two machines which could produce the metal moulds. One is from Morton and Mountain Ltd and the other is from Klaus Zegveld.

NAM UK has had a long history of dealing with Morton and Mountain Ltd and much of the kit it uses at present was purchased from them. It is known in the industry as a reliable quality producer of manufacturing equipment with good after sales support, but it is quite expensive. It is based just 40 miles from NAM UK's present production facility.

Klaus Zegveld on the other hand is unknown to NAM UK although it has been operating very successfully in Germany for the last ten years. Recently it took on a UK agent who paid NAM UK a visit.

The following information on the two machines has been collected for Peter Black:

The Morton and Mountain machine

Cost of machine	£30,000
Life of the machine	4 years
Scrap value	£4,000
Production output	12,000 units pa
Materials usage per unit	0.75kg
Labour hours per unit	0.5 hours
Variable expenses	£1,400 pa
Overhead allocation	£10,000 pa
Depreciation (on a straight line basis over four years)	£7,500 pa
Materials cost	£700 per tonne

The equipment will require skilled operators and skilled workers are paid £4.50 per hour.

The estimates for variable costs and output were prepared in conjunction with Mountain and Morton. Peter Black is confident that these estimates are reliable.

The Klaus Zegveld machine

The cost of the machine is currently £28,000. However, the exchange rate is in NAM UK's favour. There is a 10 per cent chance that the exchange rate could shift before an order is placed resulting in the purchase price being £31,000.

Life of the machine	4 years
Scrap value	zero
Production output	10,000 units pa
Materials usage per unit	0.7kg
Labour hours per unit	0.5 hours
Variable expenses	£1,200 pa
Overhead allocation	£8,333 pa
Depreciation (on a straight line basis over four years based on a purchase price of £28,000)	£7,000 pa

Materials costs as for the Morton and Mountain Machine. The equipment will require only semi-skilled operators and semi-skilled workers are paid £3.50 per hour.

The estimates for variable costs and output for this machine were provided by their UK agent. Peter Black thought the agent was rather optimistic and therefore is cautious of these figures. He believes that there is a 50:50 chance that materials usage and labour hours estimated could be 25 per cent higher. Initial thoughts suggested a production capacity of 60,000 units per annum would be sensible.

Appendix 18.4 *Summary CVs from appplicants for the job of manager*

Malcolm P. Dewick
3 Dickens Close
Stanmore
Middlesex

DOB	4.12.1938
Status	Married 1968, 1978
Education	School Certificate, Bristol Boys GS
1956–61	Royal Air Force
	Qualified in aero engineering to HND standard.
1961–65	A C Dewick, Engineers
	The family firm run by my father. I felt that the company offered little future for me; my father had failed to invest in new plant and his outlook and production methods took little account of the changing requirements of the present customers.
1965–76	ACE Electricals Inc., Rochester, NY State
	4,000 employees, Eastern Division
	Progressed fairly quickly up the organisation hierarchy and enjoyed the challenging work and the rewards which it brought. My in-company progression was as follows:
	Assistant Engineer (control components),
	Assistant Sales Engineer, Sales Engineer, Sales Manager (Eastern Seabord).
	Courses attended included: customer care, sales techniques, assertiveness training.
1976–78	Helped set up ACE Electrical's UK operation.
1978–84	AMLEC, Hayes, Middlesex
	Suppliers of aero engine parts, they also provide back up maintenance services. A division of a large US electrical company.
	Engineering Director
1984–87	MPD Electronics
	Set up my own firm, employing 30 staff – to mass produce small precision parts for the electronics industry. Materials used were plastics and metal alloys. MPD failed to survive the economic recession.
1987–present	Conduct consultancy work for previous customers as well as being employed on a contractual basis by a major firm of engineering consultants.
Hobbies	Travel, member of the Pinner Gun Club, Stanmore Rotary Club

William Longdon
40 Conisborough Crescent
Rotherham
South Yorkshire

DOB	21.9.1948
Status	Married 1974, divorced 1985
Education	8 '0' levels, 3 'A' levels
	Degree in metallurgy, Glasgow University
1969-70	Worked for VSO in Central Africa. Was involved in team tasks such as constructing irrigation systems and wells, installing pumps and instructing the local people on how to maintain them.
1970–72	P J Plastics, Hayes, Middlesex
	Member of the Special Projects Team. Involved in R&D but mainly worked on special orders.
1972–75	Ellercarr Industries, Northampton
	Technical Sales Engineer
	Sold metallic and plastic parts to electrical and electronic engineering companies. GEC was an important customer. Enjoyed selling a quality product, the customers appreciated my knowledge and experience.
1975–present	Carcroft Mouldings, Doncaster
	200 employees involved in precision high quality extrusion mouldings for the electrical industry
	Technical Sales Manager
	Joined the company as Quality Engineer and moved to Customer Services Manager before taking up my present position. Regard myself as a good sales manager with a good technical background. Have successfully introduced various changes into the works, *viz*: customer care policy, quality assurance, staff training (ranging from clerical and sales personnel to craftsmen technicians). Recently set up a Southern Region Sales Office.
Hobbies	Golf and motor rallying

Geoffrey J Nethercott
14 Mendip Rise
Alvechurch
Birmingham

DOB	14.3.1955
Status	Married 1981
Education	7 '0' levels, 2 'A' levels
	HND in metallurgy, Sheffield City Polytechnic

Posts held:

1976–77   A B Smith & Sons, Bromsgrove
                 Production Assistant
                 Managed a maintenance team of four and was responsible for
                 maintaining output levels in the small pressing shop (8 shop
                 floor workers).

1977–80   Brigstock Components, Coventry
                 Trainee Manager
                 Enjoyed the varied in-house training which I received.
                 Ranged from production management on the shop floor
                 (machined steel parts for the automotive industry) and
                 production planning to commercial and sales management.
                 The promises of a career path did not appear to be
                 materialising, so I sought employment elsewhere.

1980–present   Wilkins Tools (Machine Tools), Birmingham
                 A family-owned tool company until it was taken over by the
                 conglomerate Hollingbury Holdings in 1984. The company
                 employs 750 personnel.
                 Posts held:
                 1980 Production Assistant, Cutting and Pressing
                 1982 Production Manager, Cutting and Pressing
                 1985 Quality Manager, Hand Tools
                 1987 Assistant Manager, Technical Sales, Industrial Tools
                 1990 Regional Manager (Midlands): Technical Sales

Hobbies   Gardening and DIY, recently built an extension to my house.

David Wainwright
Cooper's Cottage
Main Street
Sedgefield
Nr Bridgewater

DOB   26.4.1943
Status   Married 1969
Education   8 '0' levels
                 HND electrical engineering, Birmingham College of
                 Technology, 1965–67
1961–65   British Army, Royal Engineers
1967–present   Tattersall Engineering, Bridgewater.
                 (900 employees) Manufacturer of industrial presses. 30 per
                 cent of output is exported.
                 1967 Craftsman Engineer, Machine shop
                 1968 Assistant Engineer, Machine shop
                 1971 Engineering Manager, Machine shop
                 1977 Engineering Manager, Small presses

1983 Assistant Production Manager, with responsibility for quality on a company-wide basis

1983 Production Manager

Thoroughly enjoy my work, it offers the perfect combination of engineering craftsmanship, making a quality product and helping customers choose the right machine for their purposes. I have seen many changes in the industry most noticeably the change toward electronic control and the use of hydraulic systems.

Hobbies   Badminton, gardening

19 · Palin Refractories plc

Glyn Owen and John Patterson

Palin Refractories plc produces magnesia bricks which are used to line steel furnaces. Whilst the company supplies refractory products for other uses, eg glass-making, the Tribnian steel industry takes over 75 per cent of output. Four refractory companies supply the steel industry and Palin is the largest with a 50 per cent market share. You are the newly appointed marketing manager and one of your first tasks is to produce a hard forecast of the steel industry's brick requirement for 1991 and an indicative medium term forecast to 1995. In giving you this task the managing director made the following comments:

'Of course we are extremely reliant on the steel industry so you will need to begin by forecasting steel output. Demand for steel depends heavily on general industrial output, but it seems to me that the steel industry always does worse than industry as a whole – it grows less in boom and contracts more in slumps. We are not in the business of general industrial forecasting, because we simply haven't got the resources, so we subscribe to economic forecasts produced by the Sunbury Centre for Forecasting. You will probably find these useful in forecasting steel output, and it is company policy to rely on them.'

The Sunbury Centre has just provided Palin's with the following forecasts:

Year	Forecast growth in manufactured output
1991	+ 2.0%
1992	+ 2.4%
1993	+ 3.5%
1994	– 0.5%
1995	+ 1.5%

As part of your investigations you discuss the technology of steel-making with Palin's technical director, he concludes by saying: 'Yes, we do rely heavily on the steel industry, but it is not as simple as that. There are three main steel-making processes, and each uses different amounts of brick. In 1990 usage was:

Process	Mag Brick usage/tonne of steel (kg)
Basic open hearth (BOH)	20.5
Basic oxygen (BO)	5.6
Electric arc (EA)	3.8

'It's a great pity for us that the basic open hearth (BOH) process is obsolete and is being phased out. BOH production will probably fall by 30 per cent during 1991 and a further 30 per cent in 1992 – I doubt that it will be used at all in the mid-1990s. The other two processes should continue to be used in the same proportions as in 1990, but technical progress is steadily increasing furnace efficiency in the big oxygen converters and brick usage will decline by about 5 per cent per annum for the foreseeable future.'

From official statistics you find that BOH, BO, and EA processes accounted respectively for 9, 53, and 38 per cent of steel production in 1990. You have also found industrial production figures and steel production figures for the Tribnian economy for the years 1971 to 1990; these are given in the table below:

Year	Index of manufactured output (1983 = 100)	Steel production (million tonnes)
1971	98.9	29.0
1972	102.6	30.0
1973	103	30.6
1974	102.3	27.6
1975	105.1	28.3
1976	113.8	30.8
1977	108.7	28.6
1978	105	25.2
1979	106.5	25.9
1980	108.2	25.6
1981	109	25.6
1982	109.4	26.8
1983	100	18.6
1984	94	15.2
1985	94.2	13.7
1986	96.9	15.0
1987	100.7	15.2
1988	103.8	15.7
1989	104.5	15.1
1990	110.5	18.2

Further research reveals that in 1983 there was a long-lasting (three-month) steelworkers' strike as a protest against the Tribnian government's proposed steel plant closure policy. The strike failed and closures quickly reduced overall capacity from about 30 million tonnes pa to 18 million tonnes pa.

20 · Views of an organisation – the case of Dave Stocks and Strong Seals Bearings Ltd

Anthea Gregory, Steve Lawson
and Bill Richardson

'Hello, I'm Dave Stocks, I'm the managing director of Strong Seals Bearings Ltd – we're an engineering company in the steel industry making machinery parts. A lot of our business goes to machinery manufacturers supplying or working in the quarrying industry.

'I'm 43. I started work straight from school at the age of 15 as an apprentice machinist. I reckon I was the best machinist in any factory I ever worked – and this probably remains true today in the context of my own workshop. I can still show the men how to do it.

'I think that I was always ambitious. I was never really happy with being merely the best machinist but it wasn't until I reached my late 20s that I got the opportunity to move into a supervisory/management position – it's often difficult to promote your most productive workers, they do their jobs so well for you. Once on the management trail I kept rising up organisations' ranks. A short management development programme proved significant in helping me develop a positive approach to my life and to the jobs of managing people and presenting myself effectively to others.

'A few years ago I was appointed production director for a small engineering company which had recently been formed. I played a major role in taking it to a multi-million pound, hundreds of employees, successful situation. I was doing OK. I had a good salary, with pension benefits and a Jaguar. The job took me all over the world and helped me forge some very useful contacts. The owner/director, however, seemed to me to be doing more than OK – he was doing really well. Eventually, I felt the rewards distribution just wasn't fair enough. I think I should have had some ownership stake. I talked to him about it and he more or less said that I could take or leave what I already had. I left a lot, but I left.

'Three years ago, with a friend who is strong financially, I started trading as Strong Seal Bearings Ltd. My director colleague and I share 50/50 ownership stakes although I manage the business – he doesn't get involved. I brought a small customer base with me to the new business, perhaps £200,000 worth of annual turnover. A key issue for a new business is not to get behind, initially, in terms of liquidity. If this happens you can end up chasing your tail for ever, never really catching up. Fortunately, with some good luck and some good management we stayed in front right from the start and we have extended our turnover and our customer base each year since start up. Currently we do around £750,000 turnover. We are profitable (I'll show you the accounts later) and we are liquid (I've just checked out acid test ratio – it stands at 0.82). We also have overdraft facilities, presently unused, which give us access to another £100,000 cash should we require it.

'However, I remain ambitious. I want to get this business into a position where I can leave it to be managed, day to day, by somebody else. I'd like to move on to other similar business opportunities where I can identify small, market-niched, opportunities for acquisition. In time, we could have a number of small successful businesses with me acting as a corporate controller. Key aspects of my purchase decisions would be first, "Can we buy the premises?" – I'm happy to work for less now in order to build up a growing base of property capital (we are buying our existing premises and they are already worth substantially more than the price we agreed to pay). The second important question I would ask would be, "Can we produce at a sufficiently low cost to make profits, given the market price for the products we are acquiring?" My experience and view of the engineering business is that market prices are set for you and if you go above the market price you will lose the orders. Being successful, therefore, is easy. All you have to do is decide whether you can make to the price and then do it. Having worked in bigger business has given me experience in production costing and we have a manual information system in operation here which helps me keep track of machine, worker and factory productivity.

'In order to achieve my small business conglomerate objectives (by the way, I'm not a big business fan – growing *one* business can sometimes be a case of growing the problems without necessarily growing the rewards) I will need to create a management structure. Presently an old colleague who came with me from the last firm is acting as production manager but I'm not sure whether he is good enough. He doesn't use his initiative enough for me, he forgets to do jobs, and he isn't good at controlling the men (we have 18 people employed in the workshop). He represents a problem and I'm not sure that training will be an adequate answer. The problem is compounded because we have worked together for so long and it is difficult to demote somebody.

'My daughter does the books and we employ an outside accountant to bring things together. We don't, as yet, produce or use monthly management information bulletins of the type which keep the organisation overview (compared to the production department view) in perspective. Having said that, the workshop is the major part of the business so if I'm keeping check on what's happening there I have a good feel for what's happening overall. I don't think my daughter has aspirations towards taking a leading role in managing the business and I'm not sure that I'd want her to anyway.

'We'd also need to double turnover, profitably. I would be happy to maintain the business at the £1.5m turnover level. I'm looking to achieve this within the next two to three years. Our present customer base is wide and varied. While we have invested in specific machinery for one major product line (and this has given us some competitive advantage – other smaller operators would find it difficult to afford the investment and then catch up with our skills), nevertheless, we are too small, still, to focus on one type of product and on particular customers only. It is necessary for us to grow in an ad hoc fashion – some of our biggest present orders are the results of our taking chances on new orders of types in which we didn't previously have much experience. Also, the nature of the business is such that 50 per cent, say, of a next week's work is only located by me phoning around potential customers the week before.

'A wider portfolio of customers also makes sense to me on an "all eggs in one basket" front. It concerns me that a couple of customers account for more than half of our present turnover.

It is very important to keep the men busy, not only from a factory productivity point of view but also because the workforce in this industry expects overtime. It's part of the unwritten deal. We've done well on this score – our men have consistently earned overtime during a period, in the early 1990s, when other firms have been laying off. Still, we are always looking to next week with some uncertainty about capacity fill.

'I suppose my understanding of the industry, my contacts and my "make to the price" policy are key ingredients of our marketing/selling activities and we have been successful in generating from scratch, a good business (we keep winning new business enterprise awards, regionally). However, we don't take a proactive longer term approach to locating, attracting and satisfying *our* type of customer. Perhaps we are reaching the stage where we should give this more attention. To be honest, I hadn't really given much formal though to 'marketing' until I recently attended a management programme which addressed the issue. A key activity here is one we've just started – the attainment of a BS 5750 quality certificate. Increasingly, I can see, our existing customers and new potential ones are going to be looking for this feature in their supplier organisations. It will cost us a few thousand pounds – I already have a consultant acquaintance working on the initial aspects and he estimates we could have everything done within six to nine months – but I reckon that in some things you can't afford *not* to invest.

'People are a big problem. Some of our major contracts require particularly skilful operators – we get competitive advantage from their ability to work the machines to very tight tolerances – less skilful/experienced operators just can't make profits. More generally, the better our people are the more productive they are. Given these requirements we have had lots of problems over the past three years. We brought some people with us to the new business but many of the best operators in this industry are established in their existing organisations.

Over time we have improved the position, picking up good people from failing businesses or because they had become dissatisfied with their existing jobs. There is a lot of movement of people between organisations in the industry although quite often it's the poor performers who are most mobile. A bigger organisation down the road has just announced redundancy plans and we might be able to pick up some good people from that source. Constantly, however, we have been held back from taking on more work either because we didn't have enough people or because I wasn't confident that the people I could put on the jobs would be good enough to produce the necessary quality. Often, you only get one chance with a new customer and if the quality on the first job isn't right then you've blown it.

'Further, we have problems with the recruitment of trainees. We get lots of enquiries but they don't often translate into good, long-term, skilled employee prospects. The last trainee, for example, left after less than a month here. However, in the long run this was probably for the best. He wasn't interested in this line of work, basically, and probably wouldn't have come good. What I have been doing over the years is carrying out a "stop/go" process of bringing in and "weeding out" personnel. Presently we seem, at last, to have got the numbers right and the skills are improving. However, this is a never ending process when you are seeking growth.

'I think the men get a good deal from Strong Seals Bearings Ltd. They have had constant employment during a difficult trading era, they earn good wages including overtime and bonuses and the conditions here are excellent compared to many of the traditional workshops. Before we moved here our old factory was in poor condition and I'm sure that had much to do with our problems of recruitment and retention. This place, however, provides a much cleaner, warmer and altogether more acceptable working environment. (It also provides us with the space for the growth for which I am looking.)

'I am a great believer in training and development as a way forward for organisations and people. At a personal level I take opportunities to widen my own personal and managerial skill. I think it is important to subject yourself to new, wider drawn experiences and to absorb and reflect on the views of others. Often the benefits of management development programmes are difficult to assess in tangible fashion but, if the programme has been good and you have participated with an open mind, I'm sure the benefits are there and will flow in due course, perhaps as part of your total approach to managing. Having said that I have a basic commitment to training, it might be that my organisation is reaching the stage where a more formal assessment of its training/development needs and a more proactive, long-term approach to human resource development, generally, is called for.

'I have a particular problem in the personnel area, at the moment. My *best* machinist is also my *worst* control problem. He drinks. He doesn't always turn up for work and he often turns up late. When he *is* here he is "streets in front" of the others and to date he has been the one employee I can count on to do the highly skilled, major customer work, productively and, quality wise, perfectly. I know the theorists talk about leaders creating a culture which emphasises productivity, quality and commitment to the organisation's basic standards. I also know that part of this needs to incorporate fair and equitable working policies. But what do I do with this man? On the one hand I need his skills but on the other hand he sets a really bad example. I've rearranged his reward system, *specially*. He now gets a big bonus if he puts in 100 per cent attendance, but he remains a problem. A recent recruitee has been a good catch. He is also very skilful. Perhaps he might give me a fall back position from which to adopt a harder line with this man.

'I am tough. People have to know what they have to do and you have to control people when their productivity and that of their machines is paramount to the success of the business. Also *some* of the people who work in this industry *need* controlling. We only allow half an hour for lunch, for example. A longer break would give some of the workers the chance to get to the pub and then we might not get them back in the afternoon. This is not the sort of business where you can adopt a loose management style. I get rid of people who can't deliver adequately. On the other hand, people who work hard for the firm get a good deal from it and part of my whole approach to business is to create long-term, secure employment opportunities.

'Buying materials is an area where we can obtain cost savings provided the quality is there. This really requires me to keep an eye out for any particularly good deals which might appear in the market place and, more generally, to be prepared to shop around to see what is on offer. However, the key cost and productivity drivers in this business are people, machines and capacity.

'The past three years have required a lot of hard work but we have achieved, in a short space of time, a successful business which provides the basis for further successful expansion. A number of key tasks, some of which represent quite significant changes to our existing approach and many of which are more in the way of "fine tuning", commend themselves for the future. However, I'm sure that consideration of other than my own perspectives on my business would help me to refine (and perhaps reformulate) my views on the nature of these key tasks and the most appropriate ways in which I should set about tackling them.'